The Riverside Literature Series

# THE COMING OF ARTHUR

AND OTHER

## IDYLLS OF THE KING

BY

ALFRED, LORD TENNYSON

WITH AN INTRODUCTORY SKETCH AND
EXPLANATORY NOTES

The Riverside Press

BOSTON NEW YORK CHICAGO SAN FRANCISCO
HOUGHTON MIFFLIN COMPANY
The Riverside Press Cambridge

# CONTENTS.

The Riverside Press
CAMBRIDGE . MASSACHUSETTS
PRINTED IN THE U . S . A

# INTRODUCTORY SKETCH.

WE are told that Tennyson made his first acquaintance with the stories of King Arthur in Sir Thomas Malory's "Morte Darthur," when "little more than boy." It is certain that his interest in the tales was shown forth early in his poetical work, for in the volume which he published in 1832, when only twenty-three years old, "The Lady of Shalott" had an important place, and it is easy to read not between but in its lines a prophecy of "Lancelot and Elaine." Ten years later, in 1842, appeared Tennyson's next important work, the "Poems," in two volumes; and these contained, beside the short pieces, "Sir Galahad" and "Sir Lancelot and Queen Guinevere," the "Morte d'Arthur," which, changed in its original introduction and conclusion, eventually became "The Passing of Arthur," the last of the "Idylls of the King." Any one can read for himself the setting which inclosed the poem on its first appearance. To the reader, remembering that the Idylls grew in the end to contain twelve books, there is a special interest in a few of the lines about the imaginary epic of which the "Morte d'Arthur" professed to be but a part. They show clearly that the possibility of an epic of King Arthur, "some twelve books," was already in the poet's mind. "Faint Homeric echoes, nothing worth," he calls the books he professes to have burned;

> "but pick'd the eleventh from this hearth
> And have it: keep a thing, its use will come."

As a mere foreshadowing, it had its use ; more defi-
nitely it must have helped to prepare the way for the
first instalment of the "Idylls of the King," pub-
lished in 1859, and containing "Enid," "Vivien,"
"Elaine," and "Guinevere." Ten thousand copies
of this volume sold within six weeks. In 1869, four
more Idylls were brought to light in a volume called
"The Holy Grail and Other Poems." These four
were "The Coming of Arthur," "The Holy Grail,"
"Pelleas and Ettarre," and "The Passing of Ar-
thur," which, as we have seen, was none other than
the "Morte d'Arthur" of nearly thirty years before.
In 1872 came "The Last Tournament" and "Gareth
and Lynette." "Balin and Balan" was the last to
appear, in "Tiresias and Other Poems," published in
1885. Thus, from the writing of the first of the
Arthurian poems, "The Lady of Shalott," to the last,
a period of more than fifty years, Tennyson's mind
could never have been long without thought of the
general theme which runs through the Idylls. In
1888 he gave them the titles and the order of arrange-
ment under which they now are grouped. Dr. Henry
van Dyke has well written : "That a great poet should
be engaged with his largest theme for more than half
a century ; that he should touch it first with a lyric ;
then with an epical fragment and three more lyrics ;
then with a poem which is suppressed as soon as it
is written ;[1] then with four romantic idylls, followed,
ten years later, by four others, and two years later by
two others, and thirteen years later by yet another
idyll, which is to be placed not before or after the
rest, but in the very centre of the cycle ; that he

_____
[1] *Enid and Nimue,* which has not been mentioned in our brief
survey of the Idylls as they now stand.

should begin with the end, and continue with the beginning, and end with the middle of the story, and produce at last a poem which certainly has more epical grandeur and completeness than anything that has been made in English since Milton died, is a thing so marvellous that no man would credit it save at the sword's point of fact. And yet this is the exact record of Tennyson's dealing with the Arthurian legend."

It were aside from our present purpose, having shown how the Idylls came into existence, to enlarge upon their significance and their beauties. Each one of those contained in this little book speaks for itself, and when the reader comes to enjoy the entire series in its order, he will feel the unity and power of the whole, perhaps all the more strongly for having tasted here of beginning, middle, and end. It will be no far search for him to find critics full of explanations, many of them excellent, of the spiritual and poetic value of the work, not only in detail but in its large plan. No interpretation should proceed far without sending one back to Tennyson's own description of the Idylls, in the Epilogue " To the Queen," as

> " this old imperfect tale,
> New-old, and shadowing Sense at war with Soul."

The remark which he is said to have made to a friend should also be recalled : " By King Arthur I always meant the soul, and by the Round Table the passions and capacities of a man." Instead of looking closely into these matters, however, let us concern ourselves with the source from which Tennyson, directly or by suggestion, drew nearly all the themes with which the Idylls deal. To turn from the pages of a familiar book to others closely related to it has in it something

of the charm of meeting a stranger and finding that
you and he have dear friends in common. The anal-
ogy must not be pressed too closely; yet as the new
friend and the old both seem nearer for the unex-
pected bond, so, we believe, both Tennyson and Sir
Thomas Malory will be worth the more to us, each
because of the other.

Who, then, was this Sir Thomas Malory, and what
is his book, the "Morte Darthur," which meant so
much to Tennyson? Almost nothing is known of
Malory himself. At the end of his work he wrote:
"This book was ended the ninth year of the reign of
king Edward the Fourth by Sir Thomas Maleore,
Knight, as Jesu help him for his great might, as he
is the servant of Jesu both day and night." From
these words the inference has been drawn that, besides
being a knight, he was also a priest; but this, like
any other surmise, may or may not be true. That
William Caxton, the first English printer, finished
printing the book in the abbey of Westminster in
1485, about fifteen years after Malory finished writ-
ing it, appears to be a certainty. Caxton in his Pre-
face to the book declares that, after he had printed the
life of Godfrey of Boulogne, "many divers and noble
gentlemen of this realm of England came and de-
manded me many and ofttimes wherefore that I have
not do made and imprint the noble history of the
Saint Greal, and of the most renowned Christian
king, first and chief of the three best Christian, and
worthy, king Arthur, which ought most to be remem-
bered amongst us Englishmen tofore all other Chris-
tian kings." Many such histories, he says, existed in
foreign tongues, notably Welsh and French, and when
the version which "Sir Thomas Malorye did take out

of certain books of French and reduced it into English," came to Caxton's hands, it was most gladly "set down in print." Between 1485 and 1634, five or six more editions of the book were printed, and from 1634 to 1816 none. A few others have appeared from time to time in our century, the most serviceable for general use being the Globe Edition volume (Macmillan) prepared by Sir Edward Strachey.

Of the King Arthur and his Knights of the Round Table whose history the book tells, practically nothing of historic certainty can be said. Scholars are divided in their opinions concerning the very existence of the monarch and his court. There are those, however, who maintain firmly that in the days when history was left to shift for itself, without the aid of writers, such a king did flourish. But whether he lived in the sixth century, or some other, or not at all, whether his Camelot was Winchester, as Malory tells, or Cadbury in Somersetshire, or a place as difficult to point out on a map as Shakespeare's Bohemian seacoast, it is certain that King Arthur and his Knights did live in the popular imagination of the Middle Ages. History and tradition were kept alive much as the stories which Homer told are supposed to have been perpetuated. Bards and minstrels, in France *trouvères*, went from court to court, from castle to castle, singing their songs of gallantry and valor. No stories had more of the elements of appeal to an audience of feudal times, or gave the teller a better opportunity to let his imagination play about his themes than those of King Arthur. Of mysterious birth and death, the founder of a noble order in which the sword and the cross held almost equal value, the victim of a false wife and friend, withal the pattern in him self of every knightly virtue, this was a hero, as his followers were a fellowship, to stir every fibre of response in the hearts of the men and women who listened to their history. The listeners were not confined to England. Indeed, Brittany seems to have been the country in which the Arthurian stories first throve. Throughout France they became perhaps even more popular than in England. In Italy and Sicily, even, the tales were well known. Each country, taught by the troubadours, never loath to use the touchstone of flattery, had a King Arthur of its own. That he is not even yet forgotten as a dead man out of mind, an anecdote which Renan told of Tennyson may show. The poet had spent a night at an inn in a village of Brittany, and in the morning asked his landlady for her bill. " You are the man," she said, " who has sung our King Arthur, and I cannot charge you anything." Such a survival of reverence for a popular hero speaks more than many pages for the power his story has exerted. It is not too much to say that the many mediæval romances dealing with Arthur and his knights, and known to scholars to-day through ancient manuscripts, were so popular as practically to have provided the world for several centuries with its code of chivalry.

In Malory's day the Middle Ages were drawing near their end. But it is no strange thing that he should have known the romances of which it was written " in Welsh be many, and also in French, and some in English." His book shows that his material was drawn most largely from the great French romances of Merlin, Lancelot, Tristram, the Quest du St. Graal, and the Mort Artus. There was in truth every element of fitness in the circumstance that an

English knight, before the days of chivalry had quite passed away, should sum up for the English people in their own tongue the stories of the English hero embodying the truest ideals of knighthood.

If the good knight, however, had been a mere translator and copyist, his book could never have lived in itself and in its influence as it has done. It was his work to bring unity and order out of what was the chaos of his predecessors; to give life to the characters; to create real men and women, of traits, passions, and individualities as strong and distinct as those of the men and women we meet day by day; in a word, to do what only a creative artist, whether he knows himself to be one or not, can do. The result is that the student who would learn something of the real lives of the knights and ladies of the days of chivalry must turn to his pages; and the man or boy whose blood is stirred by tales of noble adventure in tourney and battle, of violence and tenderness in love and war, of loyal friendship and unswerving devotion to lady and king, has but to open the book of Sir Thomas Malory, and find what he has sought.

Since the book is what it is, there need be little wonder that such a mind and nature as Tennyson's felt its spell. It would be interesting to study the Idylls and the fifteenth century prose work side by side, and see just what the poet of our own age owed to the story-teller four hundred years before him. It would be found that in some of the poems many of the incidents were purely the fruit of Tennyson's imagination. Having taken his general theme from Malory, he was quite capable of enriching the story itself as abundantly as the manner of its telling. In the thought and philosophy of the poems there is indeed, as a rule, more of the nineteenth century than of the Middle Ages; nor should we complain of this practice of a modern poet telling an old tale for modern readers. Again, especially in two of the poems contained in this selection, Tennyson has adopted the incidents of Malory's narrative almost without change. It would well repay the interested reader to turn to the eighteenth book of Malory's "Morte Darthur," and read in the chapters from viii. to xx. the pitiful tale of Lancelot and Elaine as the old chronicler told it; the beauty of the story different from the beauty of the poet's work, yet in its way no less winning, the likenesses and variances between the two versions of the tale, the value of the passage as a specimen of the sturdy old English which Malory wrote, all would be felt and prized. It is a long tale in Malory, and we can but refer the reader to it. In shorter measure he tells the story from which Tennyson made most of "The Passing of Arthur," and this passage, for a suggestion of the purpose which the reading of Malory would serve, we venture to transcribe: —

"Therefore, said Arthur [to Bedivere after the battle of which they were the only survivors], take thou Excalibur, my good sword, and go with it to yonder water side, and when thou comest there, I charge thee throw my sword in that water, and come again, and tell me what thou there seest. My lord, said Bedivere, your commandment shall be done, and lightly bring you word again. So Sir Bedivere departed, and by the way he beheld that noble sword, that the pommel and haft were all of precious stones, and then he said to himself, If I throw this rich sword in the water, thereof shall never come good, but harm and loss. And then Sir Bedivere hid Excalibur under a tree. And as soon as he might he came again unto the king, and said he had been at the water, and had thrown the sword into the water. What sawest thou there? said the king. Sir, he said, I saw nothing but waves and winds. That is untruly said of thee, said the king; therefore go thou lightly again, and do my command as thou art to me lief and dear, spare not, but throw it in. Then Sir Bedivere returned again, and took the sword in his hand; and then him thought sin and shame to throw away that noble sword; and so eft he hid the sword, and returned again, and told to the king that he had been at the water, and done his commandment. What saw thou there? said the king. Sir, he said, I saw nothing but the waters wap and the waves wan. Ah traitor, untrue, said king Arthur, now hast thou betrayed me twice. Who would have wend that thou that hast been to me so lief and dear, and thou art named a noble knight, and would betray me for the riches of the sword. But now go again lightly, for thy long tarrying putteth me in great jeopardy of my life, for I have taken cold. And but if thou do now as I bid thee, if ever I may see thee, I shall slay thee with mine own hands, for thou wouldest for my rich sword see me dead. Then Sir Bedivere departed, and went to the sword, and lightly took it up, and went to the water side, and there he bound the girdle about the hilts, and then he threw the sword as far into the water as he might, and there came an arm and an hand above the water, and met it, and caught it, and so shook it thrice and brandished, and then vanished away the hand with the sword in the water. So Sir Bedivere came again to the king, and told him what he saw. Alas, said the king, help me hence, for I dread me I have tarried over long. Then Sir Bedivere took the king upon his back, and so went with him to that water side. And when they were at the water side, even fast by the bank, hove a little barge, with many fair ladies in it, and among them all was a queen, and all they had black hoods, and all they wept and shrieked when they saw king Arthur. Now put me into the barge, said the king: and so he did softly

And there received him three queens with great mourning, and so they set him down, and in one of their laps king Arthur laid his head, and then that queen said, Ah, dear brother, why have ye tarried so long from me? Alas, this wound on your head hath caught over much cold. And so then they rowed from the land; and Sir Bedivere beheld all those ladies go from him. Then Sir Bedivere cried, Ah, my lord Arthur, what shall become of me now ye go from me, and leave me here alone among mine enemies. Comfort thyself, said the king, and do as well as thou mayest, for in me is no trust for to trust in. For I will unto the vale of Avilion, to heal me of my grievous wound. And if thou hear never more of me, pray for my soul. But ever the queens and the ladies wept and shrieked, that it was pity to hear. And as soon as Sir Bedivere had lost the sight of the barge, he wept and wailed, and so took the forest."

The more curious reader may compare this passage bit by bit, if he will, with the last poem of the present volume. The less exact may be content with testing the truth of our remark about related books and common friends. May we end this sketch with yet another quotation? Though taken from Caxton's Preface to the "Morte Darthur," the serious word it speaks to his readers may stand, linking again the old and the new, as well before Tennyson's book as Sir Thomas Malory's : —

"Wherein they shall find many joyous and pleasant histories, and noble and renowned acts of humanity, gentleness, and chivalry. For herein may be seen noble chivalry, courtesy, humanity, friendliness, hardiness, love, friendship, cowardice, murder, hate, virtue, and sin. Do after the good and leave the evil, and it shall bring you to good fame and renommée. And for to pass the time this book shall be pleasant to read in, but for to give faith and belief that all is true that is contained therein, ye be at your liberty."

# THE COMING OF ARTHUR.

LEODOGRAN, the King of Cameliard,
Had one fair daughter, and none other child;
And she was fairest of all flesh on earth,
Guinevere, and in her his one delight.

5    For many a petty king ere Arthur came
Ruled in this isle, and ever waging war
Each upon other, wasted all the land;
And still from time to time the heathen host
Swarm'd overseas, and harried what was left.
10 And so there grew great tracts of wilderness,
Wherein the beast was ever more and more,
But man was less and less, till Arthur came.
For first Aurelius lived and fought and died,
And after him King Uther fought and died,
15 But either fail'd to make the kingdom one.

**The Coming of Arthur** is based upon incidents and sugges-
tions to be found in the first and third books of Sir Thomas
Malory's *Morte Darthur*. It was first printed in 1869.

1. It would be a long and fruitless task to attempt fixing the
time and place of Leodogran and Cameliard, and other such
names throughout the Idylls, which Tennyson takes, sometimes
with changes for the sake of sound, from Malory and other
Arthurian sources. It should be remembered that the Idylls
are poetry, not history.

4. **Guinevere** is accented on the first syllable, though the
metre of this line seems to point another way. It is one of the
many lines in the Idylls in which Tennyson departs with a pur-
pose from the expected sound.

And after these King Arthur for a space,
And thro' the puissance of his Table Round,
Drew all their petty princedoms under him,
Their king and head, and made a realm, and reign'd.

<sub>20</sub>    And thus the land of Cameliard was waste,
Thick with wet woods, and many a beast therein,
And none or few to scare or chase the beast;
So that wild dog and wolf and boar and bear
Came night and day, and rooted in the fields,
<sub>25</sub> And wallow'd in the gardens of the King.
And ever and anon the wolf would steal
The children and devour, but now and then,
Her own brood lost or dead, lent her fierce teat
To human sucklings; and the children housed
<sub>30</sub> In her foul den, there at their meat would growl
And mock their foster-mother on four feet,
Till, straighten'd, they grew up to wolf-like men,
Worse than the wolves.   And King Leodogran
Groan'd for the Roman legions here again,
<sub>35</sub> And Cæsar's eagle : then his brother king,
Urien, assail'd him: last a heathen horde,
Reddening the sun with smoke and earth with blood,
And on the spike that split the mother's heart
Spitting the child, brake on him, till, amazed,
<sub>40</sub> He knew not whither he should turn for aid.

But — for he heard of Arthur newly crown'd,
Tho' not without an uproar made by those
Who cried, " He is not Uther's son " — the King
Sent to him, saying, " Arise, and help us thou!
<sub>45</sub> For here between the man and beast we die."

17. The **Table Round** in Malory does not become Arthur's
until Leodogran sends it to him with Guinevere.

And Arthur yet had done no deed of arms,
But heard the call, and came : and Guinevere
Stood by the castle walls to watch him pass ;
But since he neither wore on helm or shield
50 The golden symbol of his kinglihood,
But rode a simple knight among his knights,
And many of these in richer arms than he,
She saw him not, or mark'd not, if she saw,
One among many, tho' his face was bare.
55 But Arthur, looking downward as he past,
Felt the light of her eyes into his life
Smite on the sudden, yet rode on, and pitch'd
His tents beside the forest.   Then he drave
The heathen ; after, slew the beast, and fell'd
50 The forest, letting in the sun, and made
Broad pathways for the hunter and the knight.
And so return'd.

         For while he linger'd there,
A doubt that ever smoulder'd in the hearts
Of those great Lords and Barons of his realm
35 Flash'd forth and into war : for most of these,
Colleaguing with a score of petty kings,
Made head against him, crying, " Who is he
That he should rule us ? who hath proven him
King Uther's son ? for lo ! we look at him,
70 And find nor face nor bearing, limbs nor voice.
Are like to those of Uther whom we knew.
This is the son of Gorloïs, not the King ;
This is the son of Anton, not the King."

And Arthur, passing thence to battle, felt
75 Travail, and throes and agonies of the life,
Desiring to be join'd with Guinevere :

And thinking as he rode, " Her father said
That there between the man and beast they die.
Shall I not lift her from this land of beasts
30 Up to my throne, and side by side with me ?
What happiness to reign a lonely king,
Vext — O ye stars that shudder over me,
O earth that soundest hollow under me,
Vext with waste dreams ? for saving I be join'd
35 To her that is the fairest under heaven,
I seem as nothing in the mighty world,
And cannot will my will, nor work my work
Wholly, nor make myself in mine own realm
Victor and lord.   But were I join'd with her,
90 Then might we live together as one life,
And reigning with one will in everything
Have power on this dark land to lighten it,
And power on this dead world to make it live."


     Thereafter — as he speaks who tells the tale —
95 When Arthur reach'd a field-of-battle bright
With pitch'd pavilions of his foe, the world
Was all so clear about him, that he saw
The smallest rock far on the faintest hill,
And even in high day the morning star.
100 So when the King had set his banner broad,
At once from either side, with trumpet-blast,
And shouts, and clarions shrilling unto blood,
The long-lanced battle let their horses run.
And now the barons and the kings prevail'd,
105 And now the King, as here and there that war
Went swaying ; but the Powers who walk the world
Made lightnings and great thunders over him,
And dazed all eyes, till Arthur by main might,
And mightier of his hands with every blow,

110 And leading all his knighthood threw the kings
Carádos, Urien, Cradlemont of Wales,
Claudias, and Clariance of Northumberland,
The King Brandagoras of Latangor,
With Anguisant of Erin, Morganore,
115 And Lot of Orkney. Then, before a voice
As dreadful as the shout of one who sees
To one who sins, and deems himself alone
And all the world asleep, they swerved and brake
Flying, and Arthur call'd to stay the brands
120 That hack'd among the flyers, "Ho! they yield!"
So like a painted battle the war stood
Silenced, the living quiet as the dead,
And in the heart of Arthur joy was lord.
He laugh'd upon his warrior whom he loved
125 And honor'd most. "Thou dost not doubt me King,
So well thine arm hath wrought for me to-day."
"Sir and my liege," he cried, "the fire of God
Descends upon thee in the battle-field:
I know thee for my King!" Whereat the two,
130 For each had warded either in the fight,
Sware on the field of death a deathless love.
And Arthur said, "Man's word is God in man:
Let chance what will, I trust thee to the death."

Then quickly from the foughten field he sent
135 Ulfius, and Brastias, and Bedivere,
His new-made knights, to King Leodogran,
Saying, "If I in aught have served thee well,
Give me thy daughter Guinevere to wife."

Whom when he heard, Leodogran in heart
140 Debating — "How should I that am a king,

121. A painted battle = the picture of a battle.

However much he holp me at my need,
Give my one daughter saving to a king,
And a king's son?" — lifted his voice, and call'd
A hoary man, his chamberlain, to whom
145 He trusted all things, and of him required
His counsel: "Knowest thou aught of Arthur's
birth?"

Then spake the hoary chamberlain and said,
"Sir King, there be but two old men that know·
And each is twice as old as I ; and one
150 Is Merlin, the wise man that ever served
King Uther thro' his magic art ; and one
Is Merlin's master (so they call him) Bleys,
Who taught him magic ; but the scholar ran
Before the master, and so far, that Bleys
155 Laid magic by, and sat him down, and wrote
All things and whatsoever Merlin did
In one great annal-book, where after-years
Will learn the secret of our Arthur's birth."

To whom the King Leodogran replied,
160 "O friend, had I been holpen half as well
By this King Arthur as by thee to-day,
Then beast and man had had their share of me ;
But summon here before us yet once more
Ulfius, and Brastias, and Bedivere."

165     Then, when they came before him, the King said,
"I have seen the cuckoo chased by lesser fowl,
And reason in the chase : but wherefore now
Do these your lords stir up the heat of war,
Some calling Arthur born of Gorloïs,
170 Others of Anton?   Tell me, ye yourselves,
Hold yet his Arthur for King Uther's son?"

And Ulfius and Brastias answer'd, " Ay."
Then Bedivere, the first of all his knights
Knighted by Arthur at his crowning, spake —
175 For bold in heart and act and word was he,
Whenever slander breathed against the King —

" Sir, there be many rumors on this head :
For there be those who hate him in their hearts,
Call him baseborn, and since his ways are sweet,
180 And theirs are bestial, hold him less than man :
And there be those who deem him more than man,
And dream he dropt from heaven : but my belief
In all this matter — so ye care to learn —
Sir, for ye know that in King Uther's time
185 The prince and warrior Gorloïs, he that held
Tintagil castle by the Cornish sea,
Was wedded with a winsome wife, Ygerne :
And daughters had she borne him, — one whereof,
Lot's wife, the Queen of Orkney, Bellicent,
190 Hath ever like a loyal sister cleaved
To Arthur, — but a son she had not borne.
And Uther cast upon her eyes of love :
But she, a stainless wife to Gorloïs,
So loathed the bright dishonor of his love,
195 That Gorloïs and King Uther went to war :
And overthrown was Gorloïs and slain.
Then Uther in his wrath and heat besieged
Ygerne within Tintagil, where her men,
Seeing the mighty swarm about their walls,
200 Left her and fled, and Uther enter'd in,

186. **Tintagil**, still the name of a place on the west coast of
Cornwall.

187. **Ygerne** is one of the names modified by Tennyson ;
Malory has it *Igraine* or *Igrayne*.

And there was none to call to but himself.
So, compass'd by the power of the King,
Enforced she was to wed him in her tears,
And with a shameful swiftness : afterward,
205 Not many moons, King Uther died himself,
Moaning and wailing for an heir to rule
After him, lest the realm should go to wrack.
And that same night, the night of the new year,
By reason of the bitterness and grief
210 That vext his mother, all before his time
Was Arthur born, and all as soon as born
Deliver'd at a secret postern-gate
To Merlin, to be holden far apart
Until his hour should come ; because the lords
215 Of that fierce day were as the lords of this,
Wild beasts, and surely would have torn the child
Piecemeal among them, had they known ; for each
But sought to rule for his own self and hand,
And many hated Uther for the sake
220 Of Gorloïs.   Wherefore Merlin took the child,
And gave him to Sir Anton, an old knight
And ancient friend of Uther ; and his wife
Nursed the young prince, and rear'd him with her
     own ;
And no man knew.   And ever since the lords
225 Have foughten like wild beasts among themselves,
So that the realm has gone to wrack : but now,
This year, when Merlin (for his hour had come)
Brought Arthur forth, and set him in the hall,
Proclaiming, 'Here is Uther's heir, your king,'
230 A hundred voices cried, 'Away with him !
No king of ours !   A son of Gorloïs he,
Or else the child of Anton, and no king,
Or else baseborn.'   Yet Merlin thro' his craft,

And while the people clamor'd for a king,
235 Had Arthur crown'd ; but after, the great lords
Banded, and so brake out in open war."

Then while the King debated with himself
If Arthur were the child of shamefulness,
Or born the son of Gorloïs, after death,
240 Or Uther's son, and born before his time,
Or whether there were truth in anything
Said by these three, there came to Cameliard,
With Gawain and young Modred, her two sons,
Lot's wife, the Queen of Orkney, Bellicent ;
245 Whom as he could, not as he would, the King
Made feast for, saying, as they sat at meat :

" A doubtful throne is ice on summer seas.
Ye come from Arthur's court.    Victor his men
Report him !    Yea, but ye — think ye this king —
250 So many those that hate him, and so strong,
So few his knights, however brave they be —
Hath body enow to hold his foemen down ? "

" O King," she cried, " and I will tell thee : few,
Few, but all brave, all of one mind with him ;
255 For I was near him when the savage yells
Of Uther's peerage died and Arthur sat
Crown'd on the daïs, and his warriors cried,
' Be thou the king, and we will work thy will
Who love thee.'    Then the King in low deep tones,
260 And simple words of great authority,
Bound them by so strait vows to his own self,
That when they rose, knighted from kneeling, some
Were pale as at the passing of a ghost,

244. **Bellicent,** Arthur's half-sister ; see l. 189 above.

Some flush'd, and others dazed, as one who wakes
265 Half-blinded at the coming of a light.

   " But when he spake and cheer'd his Table Round
With large, divine and comfortable words,
Beyond my tongue to tell thee — I beheld
From eye to eye thro' all their Order flash
270 A momentary likeness of the King:
And ere it left their faces, thro' the cross
And those around it and the Crucified,
Down from the casement over Arthur, smote
Flame-color, vert, and azure, in three rays,
275 One falling upon each of three fair queens,
Who stood in silence near his throne, the friends
Of Arthur, gazing on him, tall, with bright
Sweet faces, who will help him at his need.

   "And there I saw mage Merlin, whose vast wit
280 And hundred winters are but as the hands
Of loyal vassals toiling for their liege.

   "And near him stood the Lady of the Lake,
Who knows a subtler magic than his own —
Clothed in white samite, mystic, wonderful.

275. **Three fair queens**; in an article which the present
Lord Tennyson " particularly commended " to Mr. Rolfe " as a
statement of the poet's plan and purpose inspired and approved
by himself," these queens are said to typify Faith, Hope, and
Love.   The article will be found in the *Contemporary Review* of
May, 1873, and is full of suggestion.
   279. **Merlin**, typifying the intellect.
   282. **The Lady of the Lake** ; " who stands for the Church,
and gives the soul its sharpest and most splendid earthly
weapon."   *Contemporary Review.*

285 She gave the King his huge cross-hilted sword,
  Whereby to drive the heathen out : a mist
  Of incense curl'd about her, and her face
  Wellnigh was hidden in the minster gloom ;
  But there was heard among the holy hymns
290 A voice as of the waters, for she dwells
  Down in a deep, calm, whatsoever storms
  May shake the world, and when the surface rolls,
  Hath power to walk the waters like our Lord.

   " There likewise I beheld Excalibur
295 Before him at his crowning borne, the sword
  That rose from out the bosom of the lake,
  And Arthur row'd across and took it — rich
  With jewels, elfin Urim, on the hilt,
  Bewildering heart and eye — the blade so bright
300 That men are blinded by it — on one side,
  Graven in the oldest tongue of all this world,
  ' Take me,' but turn the blade and ye shall see,
  And written in the speech ye speak yourself,
  ' Cast me away ! ' And sad was Arthur's face
305 Taking it, but old Merlin counsell'd him,
  ' Take thou and strike ! the time to cast away
  Is yet far-off.' So this great brand the king
  Took, and by this will beat his foemen down."

285. **His huge cross-hilted sword**; called Excalibur.
"The name of it, said the lady, is Excalibur, that is as much to
say as cut-steel." (Malory.) In the old English metrical ro-
mance of "Merlin," are the lines concerning Excalibur : —

     " On Inglis is this writing,
      Kerve steel and yren and al thing."

298. **Elfin Urim**; it is uncertain precisely what the Urim of
the Jewish High-Priest was ; for the understanding of this line
it is enough to know that it was a bright portion of his breast-
plate, whereby especially he learned the will of God.

Thereat Leodogran rejoiced, but thought
310 To sift his doubtings to the last, and ask'd,
Fixing full eyes of question on her face,
" The swallow and the swift are near akin,
But thou art closer to this noble prince,
Being his own dear sister ; " and she said,
315 " Daughter of Gorloïs and Ygerne am I ; "
" And therefore Arthur's sister ? " ask'd the King.
She answer'd, " These be secret things," and sign'd
To those two sons to pass and let them be.
And Gawain went, and breaking into song
320 Sprang out, and follow'd by his flying hair
Ran like a colt, and leapt at all he saw :
But Modred laid his ear beside the doors,
And there half heard ; the same that afterward
Struck for the throne, and striking found his doom.

325     And then the Queen made answer, " What
        know I ?
For dark my mother was in eyes and hair,
And dark in hair and eyes am I ; and dark
Was Gorloïs, yea and dark was Uther too,
Wellnigh to blackness ; but this King is fair
330 Beyond the race of Britons and of men.
Moreover, always in my mind I hear
A cry from out the dawning of my life,
A mother weeping, and I hear her say,
' O that ye had some brother, pretty one,
335 To guard thee on the rough ways of the world.' "

    " Ay," said the King, " and hear ye such a cry ?
But when did Arthur chance upon thee first ? "

    " O King ! " she cried, " and I will tell thee true

He found me first when yet a little maid :
140 Beaten I had been for a little fault
Whereof I was not guilty ; and out I ran
And flung myself down on a bank of heath,
And hated this fair world and all therein,
And wept and wish'd that I were dead ; and he —
145 I know not whether of himself he came,
Or brought by Merlin, who, they say, can walk
Unseen at pleasure — he was at my side,
And spake sweet words, and comforted my heart,
And dried my tears, being a child with me.
350 And many a time he came, and evermore
As I grew greater grew with me ; and sad
At times he seem'd, and sad with him was I,
Stern too at times, and then I loved him not,
But sweet again, and then I loved him well.
355 And now of late I see him less and less,
But those first days had golden hours for me,
For then I surely thought he would be king.

"But let me tell thee now another tale :
For Bleys, our Merlin's master, as they say,
360 Died but of late, and sent his cry to me,
To hear him speak before he left his life.
Shrunk like a fairy changeling lay the mage ;
And when I enter'd told me that himself
And Merlin ever served about the King,
365 Uther, before he died ; and on the night
When Uther in Tintagil past away

365–400. It will be noticed that this story of Arthur's birth is
far less like Sir Bedivere's (ll. 177–233) than like the novice's
in " Guinevere " (ll. 283–295). The mystery of his origin is
the unchanging element in all versions, in Tennyson, Malory, and
elsewhere.

Moaning and wailing for an heir, the two
Left the still King, and passing forth to breathe,
Then from the castle gateway by the chasm
370 Descending thro' the dismal night — a night
In which the bounds of heaven and earth were lost —
Beheld, so high upon the dreary deeps
It seem'd in heaven, a ship, the shape thereof
A dragon wing'd, and all from stem to stern
375 Bright with a shining people on the decks,
And gone as soon as seen.   And then the two
Dropt to the cove, and watch'd the great sea fall,
Wave after wave, each mightier than the last,
Till last, a ninth one, gathering half the deep
380 And full of voices, slowly rose and plunged
Roaring, and all the wave was in a flame:
And down the wave and in the flame was borne
A naked babe, and rode to Merlin's feet,
Who stoopt and caught the babe, and cried 'The
       King!
385 Here is an heir for Uther!'   And the fringe
Of that great breaker, sweeping up the strand,
Lash'd at the wizard as he spake the word,
And all at once all round him rose in fire,
So that the child and he were clothed in fire.
390 And presently thereafter follow'd calm,
Free sky and stars: 'And this same child,' he said,
'Is he who reigns: nor could I part in peace
Till this were told.'   And saying this the seer
Went thro' the strait and dreadful pass of death,
395 Not ever to be question'd any more
Save on the further side; but when I met
Merlin, and ask'd him if these things were truth —
The shining dragon and the naked child
Descending in the glory of the seas —

400 He laugh'd as is his wont, and answer'd me
In riddling triplets of old time, and said:

" ' Rain, rain, and sun : a rainbow in the sky!
A young man will be wiser by and by;
An old man's wit may wander ere he die.

405 " ' Rain, rain, and sun! a rainbow on the lea!
And truth is this to me, and that to thee;
And truth or clothed or naked let it be.

" ' Rain, sun, and rain! and the free blossom
blows:
Sun, rain, and sun! and where is he who knows?
410 From the great deep to the great deep he goes.'

"So Merlin riddling anger'd me; but thou
Fear not to give this King thine only child,
Guinevere: so great bards of him will sing
Hereafter; and dark sayings from of old
415 Ranging and ringing thro' the minds of men,
And echo'd by old folk beside their fires
For comfort after their wage-work is done,
Speak of the King; and Merlin in our time
Hath spoken also, not in jest, and sworn
420 Tho' men may wound him that he will not die,
But pass, again to come; and then or now
Utterly smite the heathen underfoot,
Till these and all men hail him for their king."

420, 421. The thought that Arthur would return to reign in
England is more than suggested by Malory. "And men say
that he shall come again, and he shall win the holy cross. I will
not say it shall be so, but rather I will say, here in this world he
changed his life. But many men say that there is written upon
his tomb this verse,

" HIC JACET ARTHURUS REX QUONDAM REXQUE FUTURUS."

　She spake and King Leodogran rejoiced,
425 But musing " Shall I answer yea or nay ? "
　Doubted and drowsed, nodded and slept, and saw,
　Dreaming, a slope of land that ever grew,
　Field after field, up to a height, the peak
　Haze-hidden, and thereon a phantom king,
430 Now looming, and now lost : and on the slope
　The sword rose, the hind fell, the herd was driven,
　Fire glimpsed ; and all the land from roof and rick,
　In drifts of smoke before a rolling wind,
　Stream'd to the peak, and mingled with the haze
435 And made it thicker ; while the phantom king
　Sent out at times a voice ; and here or there
　Stood one who pointed toward the voice, the rest
　Slew on and burnt, crying, " No king of ours,
　No son of Uther, and no king of ours ; "
440 Till with a wink his dream was changed, the haze
　Descended, and the solid earth became
　As nothing, but the king stood out in heaven,
　Crown'd.　And Leodogran awoke, and sent
　Ulfius, and Brastias, and Bedivere,
445 Back to the court of Arthur answering yea.

　Then Arthur charged his warrior whom he loved
　And honor'd most, Sir Lancelot, to ride forth
　And bring the Queen ; — and watch'd him from the
　　　gates ;
　And Lancelot past away among the flowers,
450 (For then was latter April) and return'd
　Among the flowers, in May, with Guinevere.
　To whom arrived, by Dubric the high saint,
　Chief of the church in Britain, and before
　The stateliest of her altar-shrines, the King
455 That morn was married, while in stainless white,

The fair beginners of a nobler time,
And glorying in their vows and him, his knights
Stood round him, and rejoicing in his joy.
Far shone the fields of May thro' open door,
160 The sacred altar blossom'd white with May,
The Sun of May descended on their King,
They gazed on all earth's beauty in their Queen,
Roll'd incense, and there past along the hymns
A voice as of the waters, while the two
165 Sware at the shrine of Christ a deathless love :
And Arthur said, "Behold, thy doom is mine.
Let chance what will, I love thee to the death!"
To whom the Queen replied with drooping eyes,
"King and my lord, I love thee to the death!"
170 And holy Dubric spread his hands and spake,
"Reign ye, and live and love, and make the world
Other, and may thy Queen be one with thee,
And all this Order of thy Table Round
Fulfil the boundless purpose of their King!"

175   So Dubric said; but when they left the shrine
Great Lords from Rome before the portal stood,
In scornful stillness gazing as they past;
Then while they paced a city all on fire
With sun and cloth of gold, the trumpets blew,
180 And Arthur's knighthood sang before the King :—

   "Blow trumpet, for the world is white with May;
Blow trumpet, the long night hath roll'd away!
Blow thro' the living world — 'Let the King reign.'

   "Shall Rome or heathen rule in Arthur's realm?
185 Flash brand and lance, fall battleaxe upon helm,
Fall battleaxe, and flash brand! Let the King reign.

"Strike for the King and live! his knights have
   heard
That God hath told the King a secret word.
Fall battleaxe, and flash brand! Let the King reign.

490 "Blow trumpet! he will lift us from the dust.
Blow trumpet! live the strength and die the lust!
Clang battleaxe, and clash brand! Let the King
   reign.

"Strike for the King and die! and if thou diest,
The King is King, and ever wills the highest.
495 Clang battleaxe, and clash brand! Let the King
   reign.

"Blow, for our Sun is mighty in his May!
Blow, for our Sun is mightier day by day!
Clang battleaxe, and clash brand! Let the King
   reign.

"The King will follow Christ, and we the King,
500 In whom high God hath breathed a secret thing.
Fall battleaxe, and clash brand! Let the King
   reign."

So sang the knighthood, moving to their hall.
There at the banquet those great Lords from Rome,
The slowly-fading mistress of the world,
505 Strode in, and claim'd their tribute as of yore.
But Arthur spake, "Behold, for these have sworn
To wage my wars, and worship me their King;
The old order changeth, yielding place to new;
And we that fight for our fair father Christ,
510 Seeing that ye be grown too weak and old

To drive the heathen from your Roman wall,
No tribute will we pay : " so those great lords
Drew back in wrath, and Arthur strove with Rome.

And Arthur and his knighthood for a space
515 Were all one will, and thro' that strength the King
Drew in the petty princedoms under him,
Fought, and in twelve great battles overcame
The heathen hordes, and made a realm and reign'd.

## LANCELOT AND ELAINE.

ELAINE the fair, Elaine the lovable,
Elaine, the lily maid of Astolat,
High in her chamber up a tower to the east
Guarded the sacred shield of Lancelot;
5 Which first she placed, where morning's earliest ray
Might strike it, and awake her with the gleam;
Then fearing rust or soilure fashion'd for it
A case of silk, and braided thereupon

**Lancelot and Elaine**, under the title of " Elaine," first
appeared in the volume of 1859. The story is told at consider-
able length by Malory, and Tennyson has followed his narrative
perhaps more closely than in any other of the " Idylls." Stand-
ing just beyond the middle of the series, as finally arranged,
it strikes the first clear note of the corruption which was to
work the ruin of King Arthur and his Round Table — the guilty
love of Lancelot and the Queen. We repeat our suggestion of
the introductory sketch that the student should turn to Malory
(Book xviii. chap. 8–20) for an example of the manner in which
Tennyson and Malory throw light upon each other.

2. **The lily maid** ; " This old baron [Sir Bernard of Astolat]
had a daughter that time that was called that time the fair
maid of Astolat ; . . . and her name was Elaine le Blank "
(*blanche*, white).

All the devices blazon'd on the shield
10 In their own tinct, and added, of her wit,
A border fantasy of branch and flower,
And yellow-throated nestling in the nest.
Nor rested thus content, but day by day,
Leaving her household and good father, climb'd
15 That eastern tower, and entering barr'd her door
Stript off the case, and read the naked shield,
Now guess'd a hidden meaning in his arms,
Now made a pretty history to herself
Of every dint a sword had beaten in it,
20 And every scratch a lance had made upon it,
Conjecturing when and where : this cut is fresh ;
That ten years back ; this dealt him at Caerlyle ;
That at Caerleon ; this at Camelot :
And ah God's mercy, what a stroke was there !
25 And here a thrust that might have kill'd, but God
Broke the strong lance, and roll'd his enemy down,
And saved him : so she lived in fantasy.

How came the lily maid by that good shield
Of Lancelot, she that knew not ev'n his name ?
30 He left it with her, when he rode to tilt
For the great diamond in the diamond jousts,
Which Arthur had ordain'd, and by that name
Had named them, since a diamond was the prize.

For Arthur, long before they crown'd him King,
35 Roving the trackless realms of Lyonnesse,

35. **Lyonesse**, a portion of southwestern England, of which
Sir Walter Besant's novel, " Armorel of Lyonesse," has helped to
revive the memory.

35-55. For a vivid picture of this scene, and others in the
poem, the student would do well to turn to Doré's illustrations of
" Elaine."

Had found a glen, gray boulder and black tarn.
A horror lived about the tarn, and clave
Like its own mists to all the mountain side:
For here two brothers, one a king, had met
40 And fought together; but their names were lost;
And each had slain his brother at a blow;
And down they fell and made the glen abhorr'd:
And there they lay till all their bones were bleach'd,
And lichen'd into color with the crags:
45 And he, that once was king, had on a crown
Of diamonds, one in front and four aside.
And Arthur came, and laboring up the pass,
All in a misty moonshine, unawares
Had trodden that crown'd skeleton, and the skull
50 Brake from the nape, and from the skull the crown
Roll'd into light, and turning on its rims
Fled like a glittering rivulet to the tarn:
And down the shingly scaur he plunged, and caught,
And set it on his head, and in his heart
55 Heard murmurs, " Lo, thou likewise shalt be King."

Thereafter, when a King, he had the gems
Pluck'd from the crown, and show'd them to his
knights,
Saying, " These jewels, whereupon I chanced
Divinely, are the kingdom's, not the King's —
60 For public use: henceforward let there be,
Once every year, a joust for one of these:
For so by nine years' proof we needs must learn
Which is our mightiest, and ourselves shall grow
In use of arms and manhood, till we drive
65 The heathen, who, some say, shall rule the land
Hereafter, which God hinder." Thus he spoke:
And eight years past, eight jousts had been, and still

Had Lancelot won the diamond of the year,
With purpose to present them to the Queen,
70 When all were won; but meaning all at once
To snare her royal fancy with a boon
Worth half her realm, had never spoken word.

Now for the central diamond and the last
And largest, Arthur, holding then his court
75 Hard on the river nigh the place which now
Is this world's hugest, let proclaim a joust
At Camelot, and when the time drew nigh
Spake (for she had been sick) to Guinevere,
"Are you so sick, my Queen, you cannot move
80 To these fair jousts?"   "Yea, lord," she said, "ye
        know it."
"Then will ye miss," he answer'd, " the great deeds
Of Lancelot, and his prowess in the lists,
A sight ye love to look on."   And the Queen
Lifted her eyes, and they dwelt languidly
85 On Lancelot, where he stood beside the King.
He thinking that he read her meaning there,
"Stay with me, I am sick; my love is more
Than many diamonds," yielded; and a heart
Love-loyal to the least wish of the Queen
90 (However much he yearn'd to make complete
The tale of diamonds for his destined boon)
Urged him to speak against the truth, and say,
"Sir King, mine ancient wound is hardly whole,
And lets me from the saddle;" and the King

75. **The place**, obviously London.

91. **The tale**, the full number, as in Exodus, v. 8 : "And the
tale of bricks, which they did make heretofore, ye shall lay upon
them."

94. **Lets me** = *keeps, prevents* me ; a common, obsolete use of
*let*, as in the Prayer Book collect : " sore let and hindered in
running the race."

₉₅ Glanced first at him, then her, and went his way.
No sooner gone than suddenly she began:


" To blame, my lord Sir Lancelot, much to blame!
Why go ye not to these fair jousts? the knights
Are half of them our enemies, and the crowd
₁₀₀ Will murmur, ' Lo the shameless ones, who take
Their pastime now the trustful King is gone!'"
Then Lancelot vext at having lied in vain:
" Are ye so wise? ye were not once so wise,
My Queen, that summer, when ye loved me first.
₁₀₅ Then of the crowd ye took no more account
Than of the myriad cricket of the mead,
When its own voice clings to each blade of grass,
And every voice is nothing. As to knights,
Them surely can I silence with all ease.
₁₁₀ But now my loyal worship is allow'd
Of all men: many a bard, without offence,
Has link'd our names together in his lay,
Lancelot, the flower of bravery, Guinevere,
The pearl of beauty: and our knights at feast
₁₁₅ Have pledged us in this union, while the King
Would listen smiling. How then? is there more?
Has Arthur spoken aught? or would yourself,
Now weary of my service and devoir,
Henceforth be truer to your faultless lord?"


₁₂₀    She broke into a little scornful laugh:
" Arthur, my lord, Arthur, the faultless King,


118. **Devoir,** duty. In common speech it has become the
word on which Hood punned in " Faithless Nelly Gray:"—

" So he went up to pay his devours,
When he devoured his pay!"

That passionate perfection, my good lord —
But who can gaze upon the Sun in heaven?
He never spake word of reproach to me,
125 He never had a glimpse of mine untruth,
He cares not for me: only here to-day
There gleam'd a vague suspicion in his eyes:
Some meddling rogue has tamper'd with him — else
Rapt in this fancy of his Table Round,
130 And swearing men to vows impossible,
To make them like himself: but, friend, to me
He is all fault who has no fault at all:
For who loves me must have a touch of earth;
The low sun makes the color: I am yours,
135 Not Arthur's, as ye know, save by the bond.
And therefore hear my words: go to the jousts:
The tiny-trumpeting gnat can break our dream
When sweetest; and the vermin voices here
May buzz so loud — we scorn them, but they sting."

140　　Then answer'd Lancelot, the chief of knights:
" And with what face, after my pretext made,
Shall I appear, O Queen, at Camelot, I
Before a King who honors his own word,
As if it were his God's?"

　　　　　　　　" Yea," said the Queen,
145 " A moral child without the craft to rule,
Else had he not lost me: but listen to me,
If I must find you wit: we hear it said
That men go down before your spear at a touch,
But knowing you are Lancelot; your great name,
150 This conquers: hide it therefore; go unknown:

122. **That passionate perfection**; Guinevere thought of the king as Maud's lover of her: —
　　　　" Faultily faultless, icily regular, splendidly null."

Win! by this kiss you will: and our true King
Will then allow your pretext, O my knight,
As all for glory; for to speak him true,
Ye know right well, how meek soe'er he seem,
155 No keener hunter after glory breathes.
He loves it in his knights more than himself:
They prove to him his work: win and return."

Then got Sir Lancelot suddenly to horse,
Wroth at himself.   Not willing to be known,
160 He left the barren-beaten thoroughfare,
Chose the green path that show'd the rarer foot.
And there among the solitary downs,
Full often lost in fancy, lost his way;
Till as he traced a faintly-shadow'd track,
165 That all in loops and links among the dales
Ran to the Castle of Astolat, he saw
Fired from the west, far on a hill, the towers.
Thither he made, and blew the gateway horn.
Then came an old, dumb, myriad-wrinkled man
170 Who let him into lodging and disarm'd.
And Lancelot marvell'd at the wordless man;
And issuing found the Lord of Astolat
With two strong sons, Sir Torre and Sir Lavaine,
Moving to meet him in the castle court;
175 And close behind them stept the lily maid
Elaine, his daughter: mother of the house
There was not: some light jest among them rose
With laughter dying down as the great knight
Approach'd them: then the Lord of Astolat:
180 "Whence comest thou, my guest, and by what name
Livest between the lips? for by thy state

173. **Torre,** an improvement upon *Tirre,* as Malory called
the son.

And presence I might guess the chief of those,
After the King, who eat in Arthur's halls.
Him have I seen : the rest, his Table Round,
185 Known as they are, to me they are unknown."

Then answer'd Lancelot, the chief of knights :
" Known am I, and of Arthur's hall, and known,
What I by mere mischance have brought, my shield
But since I go to joust as one unknown
190 At Camelot for the diamond, ask me not,
Hereafter ye shall know me — and the shield —
I pray you lend me one, if such you have,
Blank, or at least with some device not mine."

Then said the Lord of Astolat, " Here is Torre's :
195 Hurt in his first tilt was my son, Sir Torre ;
And so, God wot, his shield is blank enough.
His ye can have."    Then added plain Sir Torre,
" Yea, since I cannot use it, ye may have it."
Here laugh'd the father saying, " Fie, Sir Churl,
200 Is that an answer for a noble knight ?
Allow him ! but Lavaine, my younger here,
He is so full of lustihood, he will ride,
Joust for it, and win, and bring it in an hour,
And set it in this damsel's golden hair,
205 To make her thrice as wilful as before."

" Nay, father, nay, good father, shame me not
Before this noble knight," said young Lavaine,
" For nothing.   Surely I but play'd on Torre :
He seem'd so sullen, vext he could not go :
210 A jest, no more ! for, knight, the maiden dreamt
That some one put this diamond in her hand,
And that it was too slippery to be held,

And slipt and fell into some pool or stream,
The castle-well, belike; and then I said
215 That *if* I went and *if* I fought and won it
(But all was jest and joke among ourselves)
Then must she keep it safelier.  All was jest.
But, father, give me leave, an if he will,
To ride to Camelot with this noble knight:
220 Win shall I not, but do my best to win:
Young as I am, yet would I do my best."

" So ye will grace me," answer'd Lancelot,
Smiling a moment, " with your fellowship
O'er these waste downs whereon I lost myself,
225 Then were I glad of you as guide and friend:
And you shall win this diamond — as I hear,
It is a fair large diamond, — if ye may,
And yield it to this maiden, if ye will."
" A fair large diamond," added plain Sir Torre,
230 " Such be for queens, and not for simple maids."
Then she, who held her eyes upon the ground,
Elaine, and heard her name so tost about,
Flush'd slightly at the slight disparagement
Before the stranger knight, who, looking at her,
235 Full courtly, yet not falsely, thus return'd:
" If what is fair be but for what is fair,
And only queens are to be counted so,
Rash were my judgment then, who deem this maid
Might wear as fair a jewel as is on earth,
240 Not violating the bond of like to like."

He spoke and ceased: the lily maid Elaine,
Won by the mellow voice before she look'd,

218. **An if** ; *an* is really an equivalent of *if*, though both are
sometimes used for the second word.

Lifted her eyes, and read his lineaments.
The great and guilty love he bare the Queen,
245 In battle with the love he bare his lord,
Had marr'd his face, and mark'd it ere his time.
Another sinning on such heights with one,
The flower of all the west and all the world,
Had been the sleeker for it; but in him
250 His mood was often like a fiend, and rose
And drove him into wastes and solitudes
For agony, who was yet a living soul.
Marr'd as he was, he seem'd the goodliest man
That ever among ladies ate in hall,
255 And noblest, when she lifted up her eyes.
However marr'd, of more than twice her years,
Seam'd with an ancient swordcut on the cheek,
And bruised and bronzed, she lifted up her eyes
And loved him, with that love which was her doom

260    Then the great knight, the darling of the court,
Loved of the loveliest, into that rude hall
Stept with all grace, and not with half disdain
Hid under grace, as in a smaller time,
But kindly man moving among his kind:
265 Whom they with meats and vintage of their best,
And talk and minstrel melody entertain'd.
And much they ask'd of court and Table Round,
And ever well and readily answer'd he:
But Lancelot, when they glanced at Guinevere,
270 Suddenly speaking of the wordless man,
Heard from the Baron that, ten years before,
The heathen caught and reft him of his tongue.
" He learnt and warn'd me of their fierce design
Against my house, and him they caught and maim'd
75 But I, my sons, and little daughter fled

From bonds or death, and dwelt among the woods
By the great river in a boatman's hut.
Dull days were those, till our good Arthur broke
The Pagan yet once more on Badon hill."

280 "O there, great lord, doubtless," Lavaine said,
    rapt
By all the sweet and sudden passion of youth
Toward greatness in its elder, "you have fought.
O tell us — for we live apart — you know
Of Arthur's glorious wars."   And Lancelot spoke
285 And answer'd him at full, as having been
With Arthur in the fight which all day long
Rang by the white mouth of the violent Glem;
And in the four loud battles by the shore
Of Duglas; that on Bassa; then the war
290 That thunder'd in and out the gloomy skirts
Of Celidon the forest: and again
By castle Gurnion, where the glorious King
Had on his cuirass worn our Lady's Head,
Carved of one emerald center'd in a sun
295 Of silver rays, that lighten'd as he breathed;
And at Caerleon had he help'd his lord,
When the strong neighings of the wild White Horse

279. **Badon Hill,** a battle of actual history, in which the
Britons defeated the West Saxons.

285–300. The names of these battles Tennyson took from
other pages than Malory's.

297. **The wild White Horse.** In "Guinevere" the "Lords
of the White Horse" are described as "the brood by Hengist
left," the White Horse being the Saxon symbol. White Horse
Hill in Berkshire, on which King Alfred is said to have wrought
the great figure of a white horse covering an acre or two of
ground, to commemorate a victory over the Danes, may be
seen to-day in evidence of the ancient symbol. "The Scouring

Set every gilded parapet shuddering;
And up in Agned-Cathregonion too,
300 And down the waste sand-shores of Trath Treroit,
Where many a heathen fell; "and on the mount
Of Badon I myself beheld the King
Charge at the head of all his Table Round,
And all his legions crying Christ and him,
305 And break them; and I saw him, after, stand
High on a heap of slain, from spur to plume
Red as the rising sun with heathen blood,
And seeing me, with a great voice he cried,
' They are broken, they are broken!' for the King,
310 However mild he seems at home, nor cares
For triumph in our mimic wars, the jousts —
For if his own knight cast him down, he laughs
Saying, his knights are better men than he —
Yet in this heathen war the fire of God
315 Fills him: I never saw his like: there lives
No greater leader."

                        While he utter'd this,
Low to her own heart said the lily maid,
"Save your great self, fair lord:" and when he fell
From talk of war to traits of pleasantry —
320 Being mirthful he, but in a stately kind —
She still took note that when the living smile
Died from his lips, across him came a cloud
Of melancholy severe, from which again,
Whenever in her hovering to and fro
325 The lily maid had striven to make him cheer,
There brake a sudden-beaming tenderness

of the White Horse," by Thomas Hughes, preserves many of the
traditions of the Hill, and tells of the sports of 1857 in celebra-
tion of the local festival in honor of the landmark.

Of manners and of nature: and she thought
That all was nature, all, perchance, for her.
And all night long his face before her lived,
330 As when a painter, poring on a face,
Divinely thro' all hindrance finds the man
Behind it and so paints him that his face,
The shape and color of a mind and life,
Lives for his children, ever at its best
335 And fullest; so the face before her lived,
Dark-splendid, speaking in the silence, full
Of noble things, and held her from her sleep.
Till rathe she rose, half-cheated in the thought
She needs must bid farewell to sweet Lavaine.
340 First as in fear, step after step, she stole
Down the long tower-stairs, hesitating:
Anon, she heard Sir Lancelot cry in the court,
"This shield, my friend, where is it?" and Lavaine
Past inward, as she came from out the tower.
345 There to his proud horse Lancelot turn'd, and
smooth'd
The glossy shoulder, humming to himself.
Half-envious of the flattering hand, she drew
Nearer and stood. He look'd, and more amazed
Than if seven men had set upon him, saw
350 The maiden standing in the dewy light.
He had not dream'd she was so beautiful.
Then came on him a sort of sacred fear,
For silent, tho' he greeted her, she stood
Rapt on his face as if it were a god's.
355 Suddenly flash'd on her a wild desire,
That he should wear her favor at the tilt.

338. **Rathe**, early. "The rathe primrose," in Milton's "Lyci-das," is the most familiar instance of the word. We have it in its comparative, *rather*.

She braved a riotous heart in asking for it.
"Fair lord, whose name I know not — noble it is,
I well believe, the noblest — will you wear
360 My favor at this tourney?"   "Nay," said he,
"Fair lady, since I never yet have worn
Favor of any lady in the lists.
Such is my wont, as those who know me know."
"Yea, so," she answer'd; "then in wearing mine
365 Needs must be lesser likelihood, noble lord,
That those who know should know you."   And he
        turn'd
Her counsel up and down within his mind,
And found it true, and answer'd : "True, my child.
Well, I will wear it : fetch it out to me :
370 What is it?" and she told him "A red sleeve
Broider'd with pearls," and brought it : then he
        bound
Her token on his helmet, with a smile,
Saying, "I never yet have done so much
For any maiden living," and the blood
375 Sprang to her face and fill'd her with delight;
But left her all the paler, when Lavaine
Returning brought the yet-unblazon'd shield,
His brother's; which he gave to Lancelot,
Who parted with his own to fair Elaine :
380 "Do me this grace, my child, to have my shield
In keeping till I come."   "A grace to me,"
She answer'd, "twice to-day.   I am your squire!"
Whereat Lavaine said, laughing, "Lily maid,
For fear our people call you lily maid
385 In earnest, let me bring your color back;
Once, twice, and thrice : now get you hence to bed."
So kiss'd her, and Sir Lancelot his own hand,
And thus they moved away : she stay'd a minute,

Then made a sudden step to the gate, and there—
190 Her bright hair blown about the serious face
Yet rosy-kindled with her brother's kiss—
Paused by the gateway, standing near the shield
In silence, while she watch'd their arms far-off
Sparkle, until they dipt below the downs.
395 Then to her tower she climb'd, and took the shield,
There kept it, and so lived in fantasy.

Meanwhile the new companions past away
Far o'er the long backs of the bushless downs,
To where Sir Lancelot knew there lived a knight
400 Not far from Camelot, now for forty years
A hermit, who had pray'd, labor'd and pray'd,
And ever laboring had scoop'd himself
In the white rock a chapel and a hall
On massive columns, like a shorecliff cave,
405 And cells and chambers: all were fair and dry;
The green light from the meadows underneath
Struck up and lived along the milky roofs;
And in the meadows tremulous aspen-trees
And poplars made a noise of falling showers.
410 And thither wending there that night they bode.

But when the next day broke from underground,
And shot red fire and shadows thro' the cave,
They rose, heard mass, broke fast, and rode away:
Then Lancelot saying, " Hear, but hold my name
415 Hidden, you ride with Lancelot of the Lake,"
Abash'd Lavaine, whose instant reverence,
Dearer to true young hearts than their own praise,
But left him leave to stammer, " Is it indeed?"
And after muttering " The great Lancelot,"
420 At last he got his breath and answer'd, " One,

One have I seen — that other, our liege lord,
The dread Pendragon, Britain's King of kings,
Of whom the people talk mysteriously,
He will be there — then were I stricken blind
425 That minute, I might say that I had seen."


So spake Lavaine, and when they reach'd the lists
By Camelot in the meadow, let his eyes
Run thro' the peopled gallery which half round
Lay like a rainbow fall'n upon the grass,
430 Until they found the clear-faced King, who sat
Robed in red samite, easily to be known,
Since to his crown the golden dragon clung,
And down his robe the dragon writhed in gold,
And from the carven-work behind him crept
435 Two dragons gilded, sloping down to make
Arms for his chair, while all the rest of them
Thro' knots and loops and folds innumerable
Fled ever thro' the woodwork, till they found
The new design wherein they lost themselves,
440 Yet with all ease, so tender was the work :
And, in the costly canopy o'er him set,
Blazed the last diamond of the nameless king.


Then Lancelot answer'd young Lavaine and said,
" Me you call great : mine is the firmer seat,
445 The truer lance : but there is many a youth
Now crescent, who will come to all I am
And overcome it ; and in me there dwells
No greatness, save it be some far-off touch
Of greatness to know well I am not great :

422. **Pendragon** ; this name, originally applied by Geoffrey
of Monmouth to Uther, is used here as elsewhere for Arthur.
446. **Crescent**, literally *increasing*.

450 There is the man." And Lavaine gaped upon him
As on a thing miraculous, and anon
The trumpets blew: and then did either side,
They that assail'd, and they that held the lists,
Set lance in rest, strike spur, suddenly move,
455 Meet in the midst, and there so furiously
Shock, that a man far-off might well perceive,
If any man that day were left afield,
The hard earth shake, and a low thunder of arms.
And Lancelot bode a little, till he saw
460 Which were the weaker; then he hurl'd into it
Against the stronger: little need to speak
Of Lancelot in his glory! King, duke, earl,
Count, baron — whom he smote, he overthrew.

But in the field were Lancelot's kith and kin,
465 Ranged with the Table Round that held the lists,
Strong men, and wrathful that a stranger knight
Should do and almost overdo the deeds
Of Lancelot; and one said to the other, " Lo!
What is he? I do not mean the force alone —
470 The grace and versatility of the man!
Is it not Lancelot?" " When has Lancelot worn
Favor of any lady in the lists?
Not such his wont, as we that know him know."
" How then? who then?" a fury seized them all,
475 A fiery family passion for the name
Of Lancelot, and a glory one with theirs.
They couch'd their spears and prick'd their steeds,
        and thus
Their plumes driv'n backward by the wind they made
In moving, all together down upon him
480 Bare, as a wild wave in the wide North-sea,

453. **The lists,** the enclosure; in modern parlance, the ring.

Green-glimmering toward the summit, bears, with all
Its stormy crests that smoke against the skies,
Down on a bark, and overbears the bark,
And him that helms it, so they overbore
485 Sir Lancelot and his charger, and a spear
Down-glancing lamed the charger, and a spear
Prick'd sharply his own cuirass, and the head
Pierced thro' his side, and there snapt, and remain'd

    Then Sir Lavaine did well and worshipfully;
490 He bore a knight of old repute to the earth,
And brought his horse to Lancelot where he lay.
He up the side, sweating with agony, got,
But thought to do while he might yet endure,
And being lustily holpen by the rest,
495 His party, — tho' it seem'd half-miracle
To those he fought with, — drave his kith and kin,
And all the Table Round that held the lists,
Back to the barrier; then the trumpets blew
Proclaiming his the prize, who wore the sleeve
500 Of scarlet, and the pearls; and all the knights,
His party, cried " Advance and take thy prize
The diamond ;" but he answer'd, " Diamond me
No diamonds! for God's love, a little air!
Prize me no prizes, for my prize is death!
505 Hence will I, and I charge you, follow me not."

    He spoke, and vanish'd suddenly from the field
With young Lavaine into the poplar grove.
There from his charger down he slid, and sat,
Gasping to Sir Lavaine, " Draw the lance-head: "
510 " Ah my sweet lord Sir Lancelot," said Lavaine,

502, 503.  **Diamond me No diamonds** ; a common form of
denial and refusal, often found in the Elizabethan writers.

"I dread me, if I draw it, you will die."
But he, "I die already with it: draw—
Draw,"—and Lavaine drew, and Sir Lancelot gave
A marvellous great shriek and ghastly groan,
515 And half his blood burst forth, and down he sank
For the pure pain, and wholly swoon'd away.
Then came the hermit out and bare him in,
There stanch'd his wound; and there, in daily doubt
Whether to live or die, for many a week
520 Hid from the wide world's rumor by the grove
Of poplars with their noise of falling showers,
And ever-tremulous aspen-trees, he lay.

But on that day when Lancelot fled the lists,
His party, knights of utmost North and West,
525 Lords of waste marches, kings of desolate isles,
Came round their great Pendragon, saying to him,
"Lo, Sire, our knight, thro' whom we won the day,
Hath gone sore wounded, and hath left his prize
Untaken, crying that his prize is death."
530 "Heaven hinder," said the King, "that such an one,
So great a knight as we have seen to-day—
He seem'd to me another Lancelot—
Yea, twenty times I thought him Lancelot—
He must not pass uncared for. Wherefore, rise,
535 O Gawain, and ride forth and find the knight.
Wounded and wearied, needs must he be near.
I charge you that you get at once to horse.
And, knights and kings, there breathes not one of you
Will deem this prize of ours is rashly given:

514. **A marvellous great shriek**; Malory has it: "And
he gave a great shriek, and a marvellous grisly groan, and his
blood brast out nigh a pint at once, that at last he sank down,
and so swooned pale and deadly."

540 His prowess was too wondrous.　We will do him
　　No customary honor : since the knight
　　Came not to us, of us to claim the prize,
　　Ourselves will send it after.　Rise and take
　　This diamond, and deliver it, and return,
545 And bring us where he is, and how he fares,
　　And cease not from your quest until ye find."

　　So saying, from the carven flower above,
　　To which it made a restless heart, he took,
　　And gave, the diamond : then from where he sat
550 At Arthur's right, with smiling face arose,
　　With smiling face and frowning heart, a Prince
　　In the mid might and flourish of his May,
　　Gawain, surnamed The Courteous, fair and strong,
　　And after Lancelot, Tristram, and Geraint
555 And Gareth, a good knight, but therewithal
　　Sir Modred's brother, and the child of Lot,
　　Nor often loyal to his word, and now
　　Wroth that the King's command to sally forth
　　In quest of whom he knew not, made him leave
560 The banquet, and concourse of knights and kings.

　　So all in wrath he got to horse and went ;
　　While Arthur to the banquet, dark in mood,
　　Past, thinking, " Is it Lancelot who hath come
　　Despite the wound he spake of, all for gain
565 Of glory, and hath added wound to wound,
　　And ridd'n away to die ? "　So fear'd the King,
　　And, after two days' tarriance there, return'd.
　　Then when he saw the Queen, embracing ask'd,
　　" Love, are you yet so sick ? "　" Nay, lord," she said,
570 " And　where　is　Lancelot ? "　Then　the　Queen
　　　　　amazed,

　　　　　545. Bring us, etc. = bring us news.

*1016*

" Was he not with you? won he not your prize ? "
" Nay, but one like him."   " Why that like was he."
And when the King demanded how she knew,
Said, "Lord, no sooner had ye parted from us,
575 Than Lancelot told me of a common talk
That men went down before his spear at a touch,
But knowing he was Lancelot; his great name
Conquer'd; and therefore would he hide his name
From all men, ev'n the King, and to this end
580 Had made the pretext of a hindering wound,
That he might joust unknown of all, and learn
If his old prowess were in aught decay'd;
And added, 'Our true Arthur, when he learns,
Will well allow my pretext, as for gain
585 Of purer glory.' "

                    Then replied the King:
" Far lovelier in our Lancelot had it been,
In lieu of idly dallying with the truth,
To have trusted me as he hath trusted thee.
Surely his King and most familiar friend
590 Might well have kept his secret.   True, indeed,
Albeit I know my knights fantastical,
So fine a fear in our large Lancelot
Must needs have moved my laughter: now remains
But little cause for laughter: his own kin —
595 Ill news, my Queen, for all who love him, this! —
His kith and kin, not knowing, set upon him;
So that he went sore wounded from the field:
Yet good news too: for goodly hopes are mine
That Lancelot is no more a lonely heart.
600 He wore, against his wont, upon his helm

---

583. **Our true Arthur,** see l. 151.
592. **Fine** = subtle.

A sleeve of scarlet, broider'd with great pearls,
Some gentle maiden's gift."

              " Yea, lord," she said
" Thy hopes are mine," and saying that, she choked,
And sharply turn'd about to hide her face,
305 Past to her chamber, and there flung herself
Down on the great King's couch, and writhed upon it,
And clench'd her fingers till they bit the palm,
And shriek'd out "Traitor!" to the unhearing wall,
Then flash'd into wild tears, and rose again,
610 And moved about her palace, proud and pale.

   Gawain the while thro' all the region round
Rode with his diamond, wearied of the quest,
Touch'd at all points, except the poplar grove,
And came at last, tho' late, to Astolat:
615 Whom glittering in enamell'd arms the maid
Glanced at, and cried, " What news from Camelot,
   lord?
What of the knight with the red sleeve?"  " He
   won."
" I knew it," she said.  " But parted from the jousts
Hurt in the side," whereat she caught her breath;
620 Thro' her own side she felt the sharp lance go;
Thereon she smote her hand; wellnigh she swoon'd;
And, while he gazed wonderingly at her, came
The Lord of Astolat out, to whom the Prince
Reported who he was, and on what quest
625 Sent, that he bore the prize and could not find
The victor, but had ridd'n a random round
To seek him, and had wearied of the search.
To whom the Lord of Astolat, " Bide with us,
And ride no more at random, noble Prince!
630 Here was the knight, and here he left a shield;

This will he send or come for: furthermore
Our son is with him; we shall hear anon,
Needs must we hear." To this the courteous Prince
Accorded with his wonted courtesy,
335 Courtesy with a touch of traitor in it,
And stay'd; and cast his eyes on fair Elaine:
Where could be found face daintier? then her shape
From forehead down to foot, perfect — again
From foot to forehead exquisitely turn'd:
340 " Well — if I bide, lo! this wild flower for me!"
And oft they met among the garden yews,
And there he set himself to play upon her
With sallying wit, free flashes from a height
Above her, graces of the court, and songs,
345 Sighs, and slow smiles, and golden eloquence
And amorous adulation, till the maid
Rebell'd against it, saying to him, " Prince,
O loyal nephew of our noble King,
Why ask you not to see the shield he left,
350 Whence you might learn his name? Why slight
     your King
And lose the quest he sent you on, and prove
No surer than our falcon yesterday,
Who lost the hern we slipt her at, and went
To all the winds?" " Nay, by mine head," said he,
355 " I lose it, as we lose the lark in heaven,
O damsel, in the light of your blue eyes;
But an ye will it let me see the shield."
And when the shield was brought, and Gawain saw
Sir Lancelot's azure lions, crown'd with gold,
360 Ramp in the field, he smote his thigh, and mock'd:

636–700. The episode of Gawain's trying to win Elaine's love
is Tennyson's invention. Malory says nothing of it, though in
his narrative Gawain came to Astolat.

"Right was the King! our Lancelot! that true man!"
"And right was I," she answer'd merrily, "I,
Who dream'd my knight the greatest knight of all."
"And if *I* dream'd," said Gawain, "that you love
665 This greatest knight, your pardon! lo, ye know it!
Speak therefore: shall I waste myself in vain?"
Full simple was her answer, "What know I?
My brethren have been all my fellowship;
And I, when often they have talk'd of love,
670 Wish'd it had been my mother, for they talk'd,
Meseem'd, of what they knew not; so myself —
I know not if I know what true love is,
But if I know, then, if I love not him,
I know there is none other I can love."
675 "Yea, by God's death," said he, "ye love him well,
But would not, knew ye what all others know,
And whom he loves." "So be it," cried Elaine,
And lifted her fair face and moved away:
But he pursued her, calling, "Stay a little!
680 One golden minute's grace! he wore your sleeve:
Would he break faith with one I may not name?
Must our true man change like a leaf at last?
Nay — like enow: why then, far be it from me
To cross our mighty Lancelot in his loves!
685 And, damsel, for I deem you know full well
Where your great knight is hidden, let me leave
My quest with you; the diamond also: here!
For if you love, it will be sweet to give it;
And if he love, it will be sweet to have it
690 From your own hand; and whether he love or not
A diamond is a diamond. Fare you well
A thousand times! — a thousand times farewell!
Yet, if he love, and his love hold, we two
May meet at court hereafter: there, I think,

695 So ye will learn the courtesies of the court,
We two shall know each other."

                      Then he gave,
And slightly kiss'd the hand to which he gave,
The diamond, and all wearied of the quest
Leapt on his horse, and carolling as he went
700 A true-love ballad, lightly rode away.

    Thence to the court he past; there told the King
What the King knew, " Sir Lancelot is the knight."
And added, " Sire, my liege, so much I learnt;
But fail'd to find him tho' I rode all round
705 The region : but I lighted on the maid
Whose sleeve he wore; she loves him: and to her,
Deeming our courtesy is the truest law,
I gave the diamond : she will render it;
For by mine head she knows his hiding-place."

710     The seldom-frowning King frown'd, and replied,
" Too courteous truly ! ye shall go no more
On quest of mine, seeing that ye forget
Obedience is the courtesy due to kings."

    He spake and parted. Wroth, but all in awe,
715 For twenty strokes of the blood, without a word,
Linger'd that other, staring after him ;
Then shook his hair, strode off, and buzz'd abroad
About the maid of Astolat, and her love.
All ears were prick'd at once, all tongues were loosed.
720 " The maid of Astolat loves Sir Lancelot,
Sir Lancelot loves the maid of Astolat."
Some read the King's face, some the Queen's, and all
Had marvel what the maid might be, but most

Predoom'd her as unworthy.   One old dame
725 Came suddenly on the Queen with the sharp news
She, that had heard the noise of it before,
But sorrowing Lancelot should have stoop'd so low
Marr'd her friend's aim with pale tranquillity.
So ran the tale like fire about the court,
730 Fire in dry stubble a nine-days' wonder flared:
Till ev'n the knights at banquet twice or thrice
Forgot to drink to Lancelot and the Queen,
And pledging Lancelot and the lily maid
Smiled at each other, while the Queen, who sat
735 With lips severely placid, felt the knot
Climb in her throat, and with her feet unseen
Crush'd the wild passion out against the floor
Beneath the banquet, where the meats became
As wormwood, and she hated all who pledged.

740     But far away the maid in Astolat,
Her guiltless rival, she that ever kept
The one-day-seen Sir Lancelot in her heart,
Crept to her father, while he mused alone,
Sat on his knee, stroked his gray face and said,
745 "Father, you call me wilful, and the fault
Is yours who let me have my will, and now,
Sweet father, will you let me lose my wits?"
"Nay," said he, "surely." "Wherefore, let me
     hence,"
She answer'd, "and find out our dear Lavaine."
750 "Ye will not lose your wits for dear Lavaine:
Bide," answer'd he: "we needs must hear anon
Of him, and of that other." "Ay," she said,
"And of that other, for I needs must hence

728. **Marr'd her friend's aim**, etc. = received the news so
calmly that the gossip was disappointed of her purpose.

And find that other, wheresoe'er he be,
755 And with mine own hand give his diamond to him,
Lest I be found as faithless in the quest
As yon proud Prince who left the quest to me.
Sweet father, I behold him in my dreams
Gaunt as it were the skeleton of himself,
760 Death-pale, for lack of gentle maiden's aid.
The gentler-born the maiden, the more bound,
My father, to be sweet and serviceable
To noble knights in sickness, as ye know,
When these have worn their tokens : let me hence,
765 I pray you." Then her father nodding said,
" Ay, ay, the diamond : wit ye well, my child,
Right fain were I to learn this knight were whole,
Being our greatest : yea, and you must give it —
And sure I think this fruit is hung too high
770 For any mouth to gape for save a queen's —
Nay, I mean nothing : so then, get you gone,
Being so very wilful you must go."

Lightly, her suit allow'd, she slipt away,
And while she made her ready for her ride,
775 Her father's latest word humm'd in her ear,
" Being so very wilful you must go,"
And changed itself and echo'd in her heart,
" Being so very wilful you must die."
But she was happy enough and shook it off,
780 As we shake off the bee that buzzes at us ;
And in her heart she answer'd it and said,
" What matter, so I help him back to life ? "
Then far away with good Sir Torre for guide
Rode o'er the long backs of the bushless downs
785 To Camelot, and before the city-gates
Came on her brother with a happy face

Making a roan horse caper and curvet
For pleasure all about a field of flowers :
Whom when she saw, "Lavaine," she cried, "La-
        vaine,
790 How fares my lord Sir Lancelot?"   He amazed,
"Torre and Elaine ! why here ?   Sir Lancelot ?
How know ye my lord's name is Lancelot?"
But when the maid had told him all her tale,
Then turn'd Sir Torre, and being in his moods
795 Left them, and under the strange-statued gate,
Where Arthur's wars were render'd mystically,
Past up the still rich city to his kin,
His own far blood, which dwelt at Camelot ;
And her Lavaine across the poplar grove
800 Led to the caves : there first she saw the casque
Of Lancelot on the wall : her scarlet sleeve,
Tho' carved and cut, and half the pearls away,
Stream'd from it still ; and in her heart she laugh'd,
Because he had not loosed it from his helm,
805 But meant once more perchance to tourney in it.
And when they gain'd the cell wherein he slept,
His battle-writhen arms and mighty hands
Lay naked on the wolfskin, and a dream
Of dragging down his enemy made them move.
810 Then she that saw him lying unsleek, unshorn,
Gaunt as it were the skeleton of himself,
Utter'd a little tender dolorous cry.
The sound not wonted in a place so still
Woke the sick knight, and while he roll'd his eyes
815 Yet blank from sleep, she started to him, saying,
" Your prize the diamond sent you by the King : "
His eyes glisten'd : she fancied " Is it for me ?"
And when the maid had told him all the tale

798. **Blood = kinsmen.**

Of King and Prince, the diamond sent, the quest
320 Assign'd to her not worthy of it, she knelt
Full lowly by the corners of his bed,
And laid the diamond in his open hand.
Her face was near, and as we kiss the child
That does the task assign'd, he kiss'd her face.
325 At once she slipt like water to the floor.
"Alas," he said, "your ride hath wearied you.
Rest must you have." "No rest for me," she said;
"Nay, for near you, fair lord, I am at rest."
What might she mean by that? his large black eyes,
330 Yet larger thro' his leanness, dwelt upon her,
Till all her heart's sad secret blazed itself
In the heart's colors on her simple face;
And Lancelot look'd and was perplext in mind,
And being weak in body said no more;
335 But did not love the color; woman's love,
Save one, he not regarded, and so turn'd
Sighing, and feign'd a sleep until he slept.

Then rose Elaine and glided thro' the fields,
And past beneath the weirdly-sculptured gates
340 Far up the dim rich city to her kin;
There bode the night; but woke with dawn, and past
Down thro' the dim rich city to the fields,
Thence to the cave: so day by day she past
In either twilight ghost-like to and fro
345 Gliding, and every day she tended him,
And likewise many a night: and Lancelot
Would, tho' he call'd his wound a little hurt
Whereof he should be quickly whole, at times
Brain-feverous in his heat and agony, seem
350 Uncourteous, even he: but the meek maid

Sweetly forebore him ever, being to him
Meeker than any child to a rough nurse,
Milder than any mother to a sick child,
And never woman yet, since man's first fall,
355 Did kindlier unto man, but her deep love
Upbore her; till the hermit, skill'd in all
The simples and the science of that time,
Told him that her fine care had saved his life.
And the sick man forgot her simple blush,
360 Would call her friend and sister, sweet Elaine,
Would listen for her coming and regret
Her parting step, and held her tenderly,
And loved her with all love except the love
Of man and woman when they love their best,
365 Closest and sweetest, and had died the death
In any knightly fashion for her sake.
And peradventure had he seen her first
She might have made this and that other world
Another world for the sick man; but now
370 The shackles of an old love straiten'd him,
His honor rooted in dishonor stood,
And faith unfaithful kept him falsely true.

Yet the great knight in his mid-sickness made
Full many a holy vow and pure resolve.
375 These, as but born of sickness, could not live:
For when the blood ran lustier in him again,
Full often the bright image of one face,
Making a treacherous quiet in his heart,
Dispersed his resolution like a cloud.
380 Then if the maiden, while that ghostly grace
Beam'd on his fancy, spoke, he answer'd not,
Or short and coldly, and she knew right well
What the rough sickness meant, but what this
          meant

She knew not, and the sorrow dimm'd her sight,
385 And drave her ere her time across the fields
Far into the rich city, where alone
She murmur'd, " Vain, in vain : it cannot be.
He will not love me : how then ? must I die ? "
Then as a little helpless innocent bird,
390 That has but one plain passage of few notes,
Will sing the simple passage o'er and o'er
For all an April morning, till the ear
Wearies to hear it, so the simple maid
Went half the night repeating, " Must I die ? "
395 And now to right she turn'd, and now to left,
And found no ease in turning or in rest ;
And " Him or death," she mutter'd, " death or him,"
Again and like a burthen, "Him or death."

But when Sir Lancelot's deadly hurt was whole,
400 To Astolat returning rode the three.
There morn by morn, arraying her sweet self
In that wherein she deem'd she look'd her best,
She came before Sir Lancelot, for she thought
" If I be loved, these are my festal robes,
405 If not, the victim's flowers before he fall."
And Lancelot ever prest upon the maid
That she should ask some goodly gift of him
For her own self or hers ; "and do not shun
To speak the wish most near to your true heart ;
410 Such service have ye done me, that I make
My will of yours, and Prince and Lord am I
In mine own land, and what I will I can."
Then like a ghost she lifted up her face,
But like a ghost without the power to speak.

405. **The victim's flowers,** with which the beast was decked for sacrifice.

915 And Lancelot saw that she withheld her wish,
　　And bode among them yet a little space
　　Till he should learn it; and one morn it chanced
　　He found her in among the garden yews,
　　And said, " Delay no longer, speak your wish,
920 Seeing I go to-day : " then out she brake:
　　" Going? and we shall never see you more.
　　And I must die for want of one bold word."
　　" Speak: that I live to hear," he said, " is yours."
　　Then suddenly and passionately she spoke:
925 " I have gone mad.   I love you : let me die."
　　" Ah, sister," answer'd Lancelot, " what is this ? "
　　And innocently extending her white arms,
　　" Your love," she said, " your love — to be your
　　　　wife."
　　And Lancelot answer'd, " Had I chosen to wed,
930 I had been wedded earlier, sweet Elaine :
　　But now there never will be wife of mine."
　　" No, no," she cried, " I care not to be wife,
　　But to be with you still, to see your face,
　　To serve you, and to follow you thro' the world."
935 And Lancelot answer'd, " Nay, the world, the
　　　　world,
　　All ear and eye, with such a stupid heart
　　To interpret ear and eye, and such a tongue
　　To blare its own interpretation — nay,
　　Full ill then should I quit your brother's love,
940 And your good father's kindness."   And she said,
　　" Not to be with you, not to see your face —
　　Alas for me then, my good days are done."
　　" Nay, noble maid," he answer'd, " ten times nay !
　　This is not love : but love's first flash in youth,

923. **That I live to hear**, etc. = it is through you that I am
alive.

945 Most common : yea, I know it of mine own self :
And you yourself will smile at your own self
Hereafter, when you yield your flower of life
To one more fitly yours, not thrice your age :
And then will I, for true you are and sweet,
950 Beyond mine old belief in womanhood,
More specially should your good knight be poor,
Endow you with broad land and territory
Even to the half my realm beyond the seas,
So that would make you happy : furthermore,
955 Ev'n to the death, as tho' ye were my blood,
In all your quarrels will I be your knight.
This will I do, dear damsel, for your sake,
And more than this I cannot."

       While he spoke
She neither blush'd nor shook, but deathly-pale
960 Stood grasping what was nearest, then replied:
"Of all this will I nothing ; " and so fell,
And thus they bore her swooning to her tower.

  Then spake, to whom thro' those black walls of
    yew
Their talk had pierced, her father : " Ay, a flash,
965 I fear me, that will strike my blossom dead.
Too courteous are ye, fair Lord Lancelot.
I pray you, use some rough discourtesy
To blunt or break her passion."

       Lancelot said,
"That were against me : what I can I will ; "
970 And there that day remain'd, and toward even
Sent for his shield : full meekly rose the maid,
Stript off the case, and gave the naked shield ;

Then, when she heard his horse upon the stones,
Unclasping flung the casement back, and look'd
175 Down on his helm, from which her sleeve had gone,
And Lancelot knew the little clinking sound;
And she by tact of love was well aware
That Lancelot knew that she was looking at him.
And yet he glanced not up, nor waved his hand,
180 Nor bade farewell, but sadly rode away.
This was the one discourtesy that he used.

So in her tower alone the maiden sat:
His very shield was gone; only the case,
Her own poor work, her empty labor, left.
185 But still she heard him, still his picture form'd
And grew between her and the pictured wall.
Then came her father, saying in low tones,
"Have comfort," whom she greeted quietly.
Then came her brethren saying, "Peace to thee,
190 Sweet sister," whom she answer'd with all calm.
But when they left her to herself again,
Death, like a friend's voice from a distant field
Approaching thro' the darkness, call'd; the owls
Wailing had power upon her, and she mixt
195 Her fancies with the sallow-rifted glooms
Of evening, and the moanings of the wind.

And in those days she made a little song,
And call'd her song "The Song of Love and
Death,"
And sang it: sweetly could she make and sing.

300 "Sweet is true love tho' given in vain, in vain
And sweet is death who puts an end to pain:
I know not which is sweeter, no, not I.

"Love, art thou sweet? then bitter death must
  be:
Love, thou art bitter; sweet is death to me.
1005 O Love, if death be sweeter, let me die.

  "Sweet love, that seems not made to fade away,
Sweet death, that seems to make us loveless clay,
I know not which is sweeter, no, not I.

  "I fain would follow love, if that could be;
1010 I needs must follow death, who calls for me;
Call and I follow, I follow! let me die."

  High with the last line scaled her voice, and this,
All in a fiery dawning wild with wind
That shook her tower, the brothers heard, and
  thought
1015 With shuddering, "Hark the Phantom of the
  house
That ever shrieks before a death," and call'd
The father, and all three in hurry and fear
Ran to her, and lo! the blood-red light of dawn
Flared on her face, she shrilling, "Let me die!"

1020   As when we dwell upon a word we know,
Repeating, till the word we know so well
Becomes a wonder, and we know not why,
So dwelt the father on her face, and thought
"Is this Elaine?" till back the maiden fell,
1025 Then gave a languid hand to each, and lay,
Speaking a still good-morrow with her eyes.
At last she said, "Sweet brothers, yesternight
I seem'd a curious little maid again,
As happy as when we dwelt among the woods,

1030 And when ye used to take me with the flood
     Up the great river in the boatman's boat.
     Only ye would not pass beyond the cape
     That has the poplar on it: there ye fixt
     Your limit, oft returning with the tide.
1035 And yet I cried because ye would not pass
     Beyond it, and far up the shining flood
     Until we found the palace of the King.
     And yet ye would not; but this night I dream'd
     That I was all alone upon the flood,
1040 And then I said, 'Now shall I have my will:'
     And there I woke, but still the wish remain'd.
     So let me hence that I may pass at last
     Beyond the poplar and far up the flood,
     Until I find the palace of the King.
1045 There will I enter in among them all,
     And no man there will dare to mock at me;
     But there the fine Gawain will wonder at me,
     And there the great Sir Lancelot muse at me;
     Gawain, who bade a thousand farewells to me,
1050 Lancelot, who coldly went, nor bade me one:
     And there the King will know me and my love,
     And there the Queen herself will pity me,
     And all the gentle court will welcome me,
     And after my long voyage I shall rest!"

1055     "Peace," said her father, "O my child, ye seem
     Light-headed, for what force is yours to go
     So far, being sick? and wherefore would ye look
     On this proud fellow again, who scorns us all?"

     Then the rough Torre began to heave and move
1060 And bluster into stormy sobs and say,
     "I never loved him: an I meet with him,

I care not howsoever great he be,
Then will I strike at him and strike him down,
Give me good fortune, I will strike him dead,
1065 For this discomfort he hath done the house."

To whom the gentle sister made reply,
" Fret not yourself, dear brother, nor be wroth,
Seeing it is no more Sir Lancelot's fault
Not to love me, than it is mine to love
1070 Him of all men who seems to me the highest."

" ' Highest ? ' " the father answer'd, echoing
" highest "
(He meant to break the passion in her), " nay,
Daughter, I know not what you call the highest;
But this I know, for all the people know it,
1075 He loves the Queen, and in an open shame :
And she returns his love in open shame.
If this be high, what is it to be low ?"

Then spake the lily maid of Astolat :
" Sweet father, all too faint and sick am I
1080 For anger : these are slanders : never yet
Was noble man but made ignoble talk.
He makes no friend who never made a foe.
But now it is my glory to have loved
One peerless, without stain : so let me pass,
1085 My father, howsoe'er I seem to you,
Not all unhappy, having loved God's best
And greatest, tho' my love had no return :
Yet, seeing you desire your child to live,
Thanks, but you work against your own desire ;
1090 For if I could believe the things you say
I should but die the sooner ; wherefore cease,

Sweet father, and bid call the ghostly man
Hither, and let me shrive me clean, and die."

So when the ghostly man had come and gone
1095 She, with a face bright as for sin forgiven,
Besought Lavaine to write as she devised
A letter, word for word; and when he ask'd,
" Is it for Lancelot, is it for my dear lord?
Then will I bear it gladly ; " she replied,
1100 " For Lancelot and the Queen and all the world,
But I myself must bear it."   Then he wrote
The letter she devised ; which being writ
And folded, " O sweet father, tender and true,
Deny me not," she said — " ye never yet
1105 Denied my fancies — this, however strange,
My latest : lay the letter in my hand
A little ere I die, and close the hand
Upon it ; I shall guard it even in death.
And when the heat is gone from out my heart,
1110 Then take the little bed on which I died
For Lancelot's love, and deck it like the Queen's
For richness, and me also like the Queen
In all I have of rich, and lay me on it.
And let there be prepared a chariot-bier
1115 To take me to the river, and a barge
Be ready on the river, clothed in black.

1092. **The ghostly man** = the priest, to administer absolu
tion.

1109. **When the heat is gone from out my heart.** This
seems a thought of poetry, but Malory had already written the
passage in prose : " And when the letter was written word by
word like as she devised, then she prayed her father that she
night be watched until she were dead, — And while my body is
hot, let this letter be put in my right hand, and my hand bound
fast with the letter until that I be cold."

I go in state to court, to meet the Queen.
There surely I shall speak for mine own self,
And none of you can speak for me so well.
1120 And therefore let our dumb old man alone
Go with me, he can steer and row, and he
Will guide me to that palace, to the doors."

She ceased : her father promised ; whereupon
She grew so cheerful that they deem'd her death
1125 Was rather in the fantasy than the blood.
But ten slow mornings past, and on the eleventh
Her father laid the letter in her hand,
And closed the hand upon it, and she died.
So that day there was dole in Astolat.

1130    But when the next sun brake from underground,
Then, these two brethren slowly with bent brows
Accompanying, the sad chariot-bier
Past like a shadow thro' the field, that shone
Full-summer, to that stream whereon the barge,
1135 Pall'd all its length in blackest samite, lay.
There sat the lifelong creature of the house,
Loyal, the dumb old servitor, on deck,
Winking his eyes, and twisted all his face.
So those two brethren from the chariot took
1140 And on the black decks laid her in her bed,
Set in her hand a lily, o'er her hung
The silken case with braided blazonings,
And kiss'd her quiet brows, and saying to her
"Sister, farewell for ever," and again
1145 " Farewell, sweet sister," parted all in tears.
Then rose the dumb old servitor, and the dead,
Oar'd by the dumb, went upward with the flood --
In her right hand the lily, in her left

The letter — all her bright hair streaming down —
1150 And all the coverlid was cloth of gold
Drawn to her waist, and she herself in white
All but her face, and that clear-featured face
Was lovely, for she did not seem as dead,
But fast asleep, and lay as tho' she smiled.

1155    That day Sir Lancelot at the palace craved
Audience of Guinevere, to give at last
The price of half a realm, his costly gift,
Hard-won and hardly won with bruise and blow,
With deaths of others, and almost his own,
1160 The nine-years-fought-for diamonds : for he saw
One of her house, and sent him to the Queen
Bearing his wish, whereto the Queen agreed
With such and so unmoved a majesty
She might have seem'd her statue, but that he.
1165 Low-drooping till he wellnigh kiss'd her feet
For loyal awe, saw with a sidelong eye
The shadow of some piece of pointed lace,
In the Queen's shadow, vibrate on the walls,
And parted, laughing in his courtly heart.

1170    All in an oriel on the summer side,
Vine-clad, of Arthur's palace toward the stream,
They met, and Lancelot kneeling utter'd, " Queen,
Lady, my liege, in whom I have my joy,
Take, what I had not won except for you,
175 These jewels, and make me happy, making them
An armlet for the roundest arm on earth,
Or necklace for a neck to which the swan's
Is tawnier than her cygnet's : these are words :
Your beauty is your beauty, and I sin

1169. Parted = departed.

In speaking, yet O grant my worship of it
Words, as we grant grief tears. Such sin in words,
Perchance, we both can pardon: but, my Queen,
I hear of rumors flying thro' your court.
Our bond, as not the bond of man and wife,
1185 Should have in it an absoluter trust
To make up that defect: let rumors be:
When did not rumors fly? these, as I trust
That you trust me in your own nobleness,
I may not well believe that you believe."

1190 While thus he spoke, half turn'd away, the Queen
Brake from the vast oriel-embowering vine
Leaf after leaf, and tore, and cast them off,
Till all the place whereon she stood was green;
Then, when he ceased, in one cold passive hand
1195 Received at once and laid aside the gems
There on a table near her, and replied:

"It may be, I am quicker of belief
Than you believe me, Lancelot of the Lake.
Our bond is not the bond of man and wife.
1200 This good is in it, whatsoe'er of ill,
It can be broken easier. I for you
This many a year have done despite and wrong
To one whom ever in my heart of hearts
I did acknowledge nobler. What are these?
1205 Diamonds for me! they had been thrice their worth
Being your gift, had you not lost your own.
To loyal hearts the value of all gifts
Must vary as the giver's. Not for me!
For her! for your new fancy. Only this
1210 Grant me, I pray you: have your joys apart.
I doubt not that however changed, you keep

So much of what is graceful: and myself
Would shun to break those bounds of courtesy
In which as Arthur's Queen I move and rule:
215 So cannot speak my mind.   An end to this!
A strange one! yet I take it with Amen.
So pray you, add my diamonds to her pearls;
Deck her with these; tell her, she shines me down
An armlet for an arm to which the Queen's
1220 Is haggard, or a necklace for a neck
O as much fairer — as a faith once fair
Was richer than these diamonds — hers not mine —
Nay, by the mother of our Lord himself,
Or hers or mine, mine now to work my will —
1225 She shall not have them."

                              Saying which she seized,
And thro' the casement standing wide for heat,
Flung them, and down they flash'd, and smote the
    stream,
Then from the smitten surface flash'd, as it were,
Diamonds to meet them, and they past away.
1230 Then while Sir Lancelot leant, in half disdain
At love, life, all things, on the window ledge,
Close underneath his eyes, and right across
Where these had fallen, slowly past the barge
Whereon the lily maid of Astolat
1235 Lay smiling, like a star in blackest night.

But the wild Queen, who saw not, burst away
To weep and wail in secret; and the barge,
On to the palace-doorway sliding, paused.
There two stood arm'd, and kept the door; to whom,
1240 All up the marble stair, tier over tier,
Were added mouths that gaped, and eyes that ask'd

"What is it?" but that oarsman's haggard face,
As hard and still as is the face that men
Shape to their fancy's eye from broken rocks
1245 On some cliff-side, appall'd them, and they said,
"He is enchanted, cannot speak — and she,
Look how she sleeps — the Fairy Queen, so fair!
Yea, but how pale! what are they? flesh and blood?
Or come to take the King to Fairyland?
1250 For some do hold our Arthur cannot die,
But that he passes into Fairyland."

While thus they babbled of the King, the King
Came girt with knights: then turn'd the tongueless
    man
From the half-face to the full eye, and rose
1255 And pointed to the damsel, and the doors.
So Arthur bade the meek Sir Percivale
And pure Sir Galahad to uplift the maid;
And reverently they bore her into hall.
Then came the fine Gawain and wonder'd at her,
1260 And Lancelot later came and mused at her,
And last the Queen herself, and pitied her:
But Arthur spied the letter in her hand,
Stoopt, took, brake seal, and read it; this was all

"Most noble lord, Sir Lancelot of the Lake,
1265 I, sometime call'd the maid of Astolat,
Come, for you left me taking no farewell,
Hither, to take my last farewell of you.
I loved you, and my love had no return,
And therefore my true love has been my death.
1270 And therefore to our Lady Guinevere,
And to all other ladies, I make moan.

    1250. See "The Coming of Arthur," ll. 420, 421.

Pray for my soul, and yield me burial.
Pray for my soul thou too, Sir Lancelot,
As thou art a knight peerless."

                              Thus he read;
1275 And ever in the reading, lords and dames
Wept, looking often from his face who read
To hers which lay so silent, and at times,
So touch'd were they, half-thinking that her lips,
Who had devised the letter, moved again.

1280    Then freely spoke Sir Lancelot to them all:
" My lord liege Arthur, and all ye that hear,
Know that for this most gentle maiden's death,
Right heavy am I; for good she was and true,
But loved me with a love beyond all love
1285 In woman, whomsoever I have known.
Yet to be loved makes not to love again;
Not at my years, however it hold in youth.
I swear by truth and knighthood that I gave
No cause, not willingly, for such a love:
1290 To this I call my friends in testimony,
Her brethren, and her father, who himself
Besought me to be plain and blunt, and use,
To break her passion, some discourtesy
Against my nature: what I could, I did.
1295 I left her and I bade her no farewell;
Tho', had I dreamt the damsel would have died,
I might have put my wits to some rough use,
And help'd her from herself."

                              Then said the Queen
(Sea was her wrath, yet working after storm)
1300 " Ye might at least have done her so much grace,

Fair lord, as would have help'd her from her
    death."
He raised his head, their eyes met and hers fell,
He adding :

       " Queen, she would not be content
Save that I wedded her, which could not be.
1305 Then might she follow me thro' the world, she
    ask'd ;
It could not be. I told her that her love
Was but the flash of youth, would darken down
To rise hereafter in a stiller flame
Toward one more worthy of her — then would I,
1310 More specially were he she wedded poor,
Estate them with large land and territory
In mine own realm beyond the narrow seas,
To keep them in all joyance : more than this
I could not ; this she would not, and she died."

1315 He pausing, Arthur answer'd, " O my knight,
It will be to thy worship, as my knight,
And mine, as head of all our Table Round,
To see that she be buried worshipfully."

So toward that shrine which then in all the realm
1320 Was richest, Arthur leading, slowly went
The marshall'd Order of their Table Round,
And Lancelot sat beyond his wont, to see
The maiden buried, not as one unknown,
Nor meanly, but with gorgeous obsequies,

1319. **That shrine,** presumably Westminster, as Malory's
narrative of the bringing of Elaine to the court reads: " And
30 the man steared the barget unto Westminster, and there he
rowed a great while to and fro as any espied it."

1325 And mass, and rolling music, like a queen.
  And when the knights had laid her comely head
  Low in the dust of half-forgotten kings,
  Then Arthur spake among them, " Let her tomb
  Be costly, and her image thereupon,
1330 And let the shield of Lancelot at her feet
  Be carven, and her lily in her hand.
  And let the story of her dolorous voyage
  For all true hearts be blazon'd on her tomb
  In letters gold and azure ! " which was wrought
1335 Thereafter ; but when now the lords and dames
  And people, from the high door streaming, brake
  Disorderly, as homeward each, the Queen,
  Who mark'd Sir Lancelot where he moved apart,
  Drew near, and sigh'd in passing, " Lancelot,
1340 Forgive me ; mine was jealousy in love."
  He answer'd with his eyes upon the ground,
  " That is love's curse ; pass on, my Queen, for
      given."
  But Arthur, who beheld his cloudy brows,
  Approach'd him, and with full affection said,

1345    " Lancelot, my Lancelot, thou in whom I have
  Most joy and most affiance, for I know
  What thou hast been in battle by my side,
  And many a time have watch'd thee at the tilt
  Strike down the lusty and long-practised knight,
1350 And let the younger and unskill'd go by
  To win his honor and to make his name,
  And loved thy courtesies and thee, a man
  Made to be loved ; but now I would to God,
  Seeing the homeless trouble in thine eyes,
1355 Thou couldst have loved this maiden, shaped, it
      seems,

By God for thee alone, and from her face,
If one may judge the living by the dead,
Delicately pure and marvellously fair,
Who might have brought thee, now a lonely man,
360 Wifeless and heirless, noble issue, sons
Born to the glory of thy name and fame,
My knight, the great Sir Lancelot of the Lake."

Then answer'd Lancelot, "Fair she was, my
King,
Pure, as you ever wish your knights to be.
1365 To doubt her fairness were to want an eye,
To doubt her pureness were to want a heart —
Yea, to be loved, if what is worthy love
Could bind him, but free love will not be bound."

"Free love, so bound, were freëst," said the
King.
1370 "Let love be free; free love is for the best:
And, after heaven, on our dull side of death,
What should be best, if not so pure a love
Clothed in so pure a loveliness? yet thee
She fail'd to bind, tho' being, as I think,
1375 Unbound as yet, and gentle, as I know."

And Lancelot answer'd nothing, but he went,
And at the inrunning of a little brook
Sat by the river in a cove, and watch'd
The high reed wave, and lifted up his eyes
1380 And saw the barge that brought her moving down,
Far-off, a blot upon the stream, and said
Low in himself, "Ah simple heart and sweet,
Ye loved me, damsel, surely with a love
Far tenderer than my Queen's. Pray for thy soul?

1385 Ay, that will I. Farewell too — now at last —
Farewell, fair lily. 'Jealousy in love?'
Not rather dead love's harsh heir, jealous pride?
Queen, if I grant the jealousy as of love,
May not your crescent fear for name and fame,
1390 Speak, as it waxes, of a love that wanes?
Why did the King dwell on my name to me?
Mine own name shames me, seeming a reproach,
Lancelot, whom the Lady of the Lake
Caught from his mother's arms — the wondrous one
1395 Who passes thro' the vision of the night —
She chanted snatches of mysterious hymns
Heard on the winding waters, eve and morn.
She kiss'd me saying, 'Thou art fair, my child,
As a king's son,' and often in her arms
1400 She bare me, pacing on the dusky mere.
Would she had drown'd me in it, where'er it be!
For what am I? what profits me my name
Of greatest knight? I fought for it, and have it:
Pleasure to have it, none; to lose it, pain;
1405 Now grown a part of me: but what use in it?
To make men worse by making my sin known?
Or sin seem less, the sinner seeming great?
Alas for Arthur's greatest knight, a man
Not after Arthur's heart! I needs must break
1410 These bonds that so defame me: not without
She wills it: would I, if she will'd it? nay,
Who knows? but if I would not, then may God,
I pray him, send a sudden Angel down
To seize me by the hair and bear me far,
1415 And fling me deep in that forgotten mere,
Among the tumbled fragments of the hills."

1389. **Crescent**; see l. 446.
1391. **My name**, meaning also *my fame*.

So groaned Sir Lancelot in remorseful pain,
Not knowing he should die a holy man.


# GUINEVERE.

QUEEN GUINEVERE had fled the court, and sat
There in the holy house at Almesbury

1418. **A holy man**; according to Malory, Lancelot, after the death of Arthur, enters the hermitage where the remnant of his fellow-knights also dwelt. There, after the death of Guinevere, he died. Sir Ector's lament over his body is one of the noblest passages in Malory's book : " Ah, Launcelot, he said, thou were head of all Christian knights ; and now I dare say, said Sir Ecter, thou Sir Launcelot, there thou liest, that thou were never matched of earthly knight's hand ; and thou were the courtiest knight that ever bare shield ; and thou were the truest friend to thy lover that ever bestrode horse ; and thou were the truest lover of a sinful man that ever loved woman ; and thou were the kindest man that ever strake with sword ; and thou were the goodliest person that ever came among press of knights ; and thou was the meekest man and the gentlest that ever ate in hall among ladies ; and thou were the sternest knight to thy mortal foe that ever put spear in the rest."

**Guinevere**, like "Lancelot and Elaine," first appeared in the volume of 1859. The story is Tennyson's, except for a few suggestions taken from Malory. The queen, in the old story, did enter the nunnery at Almesbury, but not until after Arthur's death, and it was Lancelot, not Arthur, who went to see her there. In many details, also, there are variances.

For its personal interest it is worth while to insert a portion of Bayard Taylor's account of a visit to Tennyson, and of the poet's reading of "Guinevere" after dinner : " His reading is a strange monotonous chant, with unexpected falling inflexions, which I cannot describe, but can imitate exactly. It is very impressive. In spite of myself I became very much excited as he went on. Finally, when Arthur forgives the Queen, Tennyson's voice fairly broke. I found tears on my cheeks, and Mr. and Mrs. Tennyson were crying, one on either side of me. He

Weeping, none with her save a little maid,
A novice: one low light betwixt them burn'd
5 Blurr'd by the creeping mist, for all abroad,
Beneath a moon unseen albeit at full,
The white mist, like a face-cloth to the face,
Clung to the dead earth, and the land was still.

For hither had she fled, her cause of flight
10 Sir Modred; he that like a subtle beast
Lay couchant with his eyes upon the throne,
Ready to spring, waiting a chance: for this
He chill'd the popular praises of the King
With silent smiles of slow disparagement;
15 And tampered with the Lords of the White Horse,
Heathen, the brood by Hengist left: and sought
To make disruption in the Table Round
Of Arthur, and to splinter it into feuds
Serving his traitorous end; and all his aims
20 Were sharpen'd by strong hate for Lancelot.

For thus it chanced one morn when all the court,
Green-suited, but with plumes that mock'd the may,
Had been, their wont, a-maying and return'd,
That Modred still in green, all ear and eye,
25 Climb'd to the high top of the garden-wall
To spy some secret scandal if he might,

made an effort, and went on to the end, closing grandly. 'How
can you say,' I asked (referring to the previous conversation),
'that you have no surety of permanent fame? This poem will
only die with the language in which it is written.' Mrs. Tenny-
son started up from her couch, 'It is true!' she exclaimed; 'I
have told Alfred the same thing.'"

15. **Lords of the White Horse**; see "Lancelot and Elaine,"
l. 297, note.

22. **The may** = the hawthorn-flower.

And saw the Queen who sat betwixt her best
Enid, and lissome Vivien, of her court
The wiliest and the worst; and more than this
30 He saw not, for Sir Lancelot passing by
Spied where he couch'd, and as the gardener's hand
Picks from the colewort a green caterpillar,
So from the high wall and the flowering grove
Of grasses Lancelot pluck'd him by the heel,
35 And cast him as a worm upon the way;
But when he knew the Prince tho' marr'd with dust,
He, reverencing king's blood in a bad man,
Made such excuses as he might, and these
Full knightly without scorn; for in those days
40 No knight of Arthur's noblest dealt in scorn;
But, if a man were halt or hunch'd, in him
By those whom God had made full-limb'd and tall,
Scorn was allow'd as part of his defect,
And he was answer'd softly by the King
45 And all his Table. So Sir Lancelot holp
To raise the Prince, who rising twice or thrice
Full sharply smote his knees, and smiled, and went:
But, ever after, the small violence done
Rankled in him and ruffled all his heart,
50 As the sharp wind that ruffles all day long
A little bitter pool about a stone
On the bare coast.

But when Sir Lancelot told
This matter to the Queen, at first she laugh'd
Lightly, to think of Modred's dusty fall,
55 Then shudder'd, as the village wife who cries
" I shudder, some one steps across my grave; "
Then laugh'd again, but faintlier, for indeed
She half-foresaw that he, the subtle beast,

Would track her guilt until he found, and hers
60 Would be for evermore a name of scorn.
Henceforward rarely could she front in hall,
Or elsewhere, Modred's narrow foxy face,
Heart-hiding smile, and gray persistent eye:
Henceforward too, the Powers that tend the soul,
65 To help it from the death that cannot die,
And save it even in extremes, began
To vex and plague her. Many a time for hours,
Beside the placid breathings of the King,
In the dead night, grim faces came and went
70 Before her, or a vague spiritual fear —
Like to some doubtful noise of creaking doors,
Heard by the watcher in a haunted house,
That keeps the rust of murder on the walls —
Held her awake: or if she slept, she dream'd
75 An awful dream; for then she seemed to stand
On some vast plain before a setting sun,
And from the sun there swiftly made at her
A ghastly something, and its shadow flew
Before it till it touch'd her, and she turn'd —
80 When lo! her own, that broadening from her feet,
And blackening, swallow'd all the land, and in it
Far cities burnt, and with a cry she woke.
And all this trouble did not pass but grew;
Till ev'n the clear face of the guileless King,
85 And trustful courtesies of household life,
Became her bane; and at the last she said,
"O Lancelot, get thee hence to thine own land,
For if thou tarry we shall meet again,
And if we meet again, some evil chance
90 Will make the smouldering scandal break and blaze
Before the people, and our lord the King."
And Lancelot ever promised, but remain'd,

And still they met and met.   Again she said,
" O Lancelot, if thou love me get thee hence."
35 And then they were agreed upon a night
(When the good King should not be there) to meet
And part for ever.   Passion-pale they met
And greeted: hands in hands, and eye to eye,
Low on the border of her couch they sat
100 Stammering and staring: it was their last hour,
A madness of farewells.   And Modred brought
His creatures to the basement of the tower
For testimony; and crying with full voice
"Traitor, come out, ye are trapt at last," aroused
105 Lancelot, who rushing outward lionlike
Leapt on him, and hurl'd him headlong, and he fell
Stunn'd, and his creatures took and bare him off,
And all was still: then she, " The end is come,
And I am shamed for ever;" and he said:
110 " Mine be the shame; mine was the sin: but rise,
And fly to my strong castle overseas:
There will I hide thee till my life shall end,
There hold thee with my life against the world."
She answer'd: " Lancelot, wilt thou hold me so?
115 Nay, friend, for we have taken our farewells.
Would God that thou couldst hide me from myself!
Mine is the shame, for I was wife, and thou
Unwedded: yet rise now, and let us fly,
For I will draw me into sanctuary,
120 And bide my doom."   So Lancelot got her horse,
Set her thereon, and mounted on his own,
And then they rode to the divided way,

119. **Into sanctuary**, for protection.

120–143. In Malory the queen fled with Lancelot to his castle of Joyous Gard, after he had rescued her from death at the stake for her sins.

There kiss'd, and parted weeping: for he past,
Love-loyal to the least wish of the Queen,
125 Back to his land; but she to Almesbury
Fled all night long by glimmering waste and weald,
And heard the Spirits of the waste and weald
Moan as she fled, or thought she heard them
        moan:
And in herself she moan'd "Too late, too late!"
130 Till in the cold wind that foreruns the morn,
A blot in heaven, the Raven, flying high,
Croak'd, and she thought, "He spies a field of
        death;
For now the Heathen of the Northern Sea,
Lured by the crimes and frailties of the court,
135 Begin to slay the folk, and spoil the land."

And when she came to Almesbury she spake
There to the nuns, and said, "Mine enemies
Pursue me, but, O peaceful Sisterhood,
Receive, and yield me sanctuary, nor ask
140 Her name to whom ye yield it, till her time
To tell you:" and her beauty, grace and power,
Wrought as a charm upon them, and they spared
To ask it.

                So the stately Queen abode
For many a week, unknown, among the nuns;
145 Nor with them mix'd, nor told her name, nor sought,
Wrapt in her grief, for housel or for shrift,
But communed only with the little maid,
Who pleased her with a babbling heedlessness
Which often lured her from herself; but now,
150 This night, a rumor wildly blown about
Came, that Sir Modred had usurp'd the realm,

And leagued him with the heathen, while the King
Was waging war on Lancelot : then she thought,
" With what a hate the people and the King
155 Must hate me," and bow'd down upon her hands
Silent, until the little maid, who brook'd
No silence, brake it, uttering " Late ! so late !
What hour, I wonder, now ? " and when she drew
No answer, by and by began to hum
160 An air the nuns had taught her : " Late, so late ! "
Which when she heard, the Queen look'd up, and
    said,
" O maiden, if indeed ye list to sing,
Sing, and unbind my heart that I may weep."
Whereat full willingly sang the little maid :

165   " Late, late, so late ! and dark the night and
        chill !
Late, late, so late ! but we can enter still.
Too late, too late ! ye cannot enter now.

  " No light had we : for that we do repent ;
And learning this, the bridegroom will relent.
170 Too late, too late ! ye cannot enter now.

  " No light : so late ! and dark and chill the night !
O let us in, that we may find the light !
Too late, too late : ye cannot enter now.

  " Have we not heard the bridegroom is so sweet ?
175 O let us in, tho' late, to kiss his feet !
No, no, too late ! ye cannot enter now."

165. **Late, late, so late**; the reader will recall Elaine's
" Song of Love and Death " (l. 1000), close of kin to these lines
in beauty and structure.

So sang the novice, while full passionately,
Her head upon her hands, remembering
Her thought when first she came, wept the **sad**
      Queen.

180 Then said the little novice prattling to her :

      "O pray you, noble lady, weep no more ;
But let my words, the words of one so small,
Who knowing nothing knows but to obey,
And if I do not there is penance given —
185 Comfort your sorrows ; for they do not flow
From evil done ; right sure am I of that,
Who see your tender grace and stateliness.
But weigh your sorrows with our lord the King's,
And weighing find them less ; for gone is he
190 To wage grim war against Sir Lancelot there,
Round that strong castle where he holds the Queen ;
And Modred whom he left in charge of all,
The traitor —   Ah sweet lady, the King's grief
For his own self, and his own Queen, and realm,
195 Must needs be thrice as great as any of ours.
For me, I thank the saints, I am not great ;
For if there ever come a grief to me
I cry my cry in silence, and have done.
None knows it, and my tears have brought me good.
200 But even were the griefs of little ones
As great as those of great ones, yet this grief
Is added to the griefs the great must bear,
That howsoever much they may desire
Silence, they cannot weep behind a cloud :

179. **Her thought,** see l. 129.
191. **Where he holds the Queen** ; it was evidently the
popular belief, in Tennyson's scheme of the story, that the queen
was with Lancelot, as Malory says she was.

105 As even here they talk at Almesbury
About the good King and his wicked Queen,
And were I such a King with such a Queen,
Well might I wish to veil her wickedness,
But were I such a King, it could not be."

110    Then to her own sad heart mutter'd the Queen,
" Will the child kill me with her innocent talk ?"
But openly she answer'd, " Must not I,
If this false traitor have displaced his lord,
Grieve with the common grief of all the realm ? "

215    " Yea," said the maid, " this is all woman's grief,
That *she* is woman, whose disloyal life
Hath wrought confusion in the Table Round
Which good King Arthur founded, years ago,
With signs and miracles and wonders, there
220 At Camelot, ere the coming of the Queen."

Then thought the Queen within herself again,
" Will the child kill me with her foolish prate ? "
But openly she spake and said to her,
" O little maid, shut in by nunnery walls,
225 What canst thou know of Kings and Tables Round,
Or what of signs and wonders, but the signs
And simple miracles of thy nunnery ? "

To whom the little novice garrulously,
" Yea, but I know: the land was full of signs
230 And wonders ere the coming of the Queen.
So said my father, and himself was knight
Of the great Table — at the founding of it ;
And rode thereto from Lyonnesse, and he said

233. **Lyonesse;** see " Lancelot and Elaine," l. 35, note.

That as he rode, an hour or maybe twain
235 After the sunset, down the coast, he heard
Strange music, and he paused, and turning — there,
All down the lonely coast of Lyonnesse,
Each with a beacon star upon his head,
And with a wild sea-light about his feet,
240 He saw them — headland after headland flame
Far on into the rich heart of the west :
And in the light the white mermaiden swam,
And strong man-breasted things stood from the sea,
And sent a deep sea-voice thro' all the land,
245 To which the little elves of chasm and cleft
Made answer, sounding like a distant horn.
So said my father — yea, and furthermore,
Next morning, while he past the dim-lit woods,
Himself beheld three spirits mad with joy
250 Come dashing down on a tall wayside flower,
That shook beneath them, as the thistle shakes
When three gray linnets wrangle for the seed :
And still at evenings on before his horse
The flickering fairy-circle wheel'd and broke
255 Flying, and link'd again, and wheel'd and broke
Flying, for all the land was full of life.
And when at last he came to Camelot,
A wreath of airy dancers hand-in-hand
Swung round the lighted lantern of the hall ;
260 And in the hall itself was such a feast
As never man had dream'd ; for every knight
Had whatsoever meat he long'd for served
By hands unseen ; and even as he said
Down in the cellars merry bloated things
265 Shoulder'd the spigot, straddling on the butts
While the wine ran : so glad were spirits and men
Before the coming of the sinful Queen."

Then spake the Queen and somewhat bitterly,
"Were they so glad? ill prophets were they all,
Spirits and men: could none of them foresee,
Not even thy wise father with his signs
And wonders, what has fall'n upon the realm?"

To whom the novice garrulously again,
"Yea, one, a bard; of whom my father said,
Full many a noble war-song had he sung,
Ev'n in the presence of an enemy's fleet,
Between the steep cliff and the coming wave;
And many a mystic lay of life and death
Had chanted on the smoky mountain-tops,
When round him bent the spirits of the hills
With all their dewy hair blown back like flame:
So said my father — and that night the bard
Sang Arthur's glorious wars, and sang the King
As wellnigh more than man, and rail'd at those
Who call'd him the false son of Gorloïs:
For there was no man knew from whence he came;
But after tempest, when the long wave broke
All down the thundering shores of Bude and Bos,
There came a day as still as heaven, and then
They found a naked child upon the sands
Of dark Tintagil by the Cornish sea;
And that was Arthur; and they foster'd him
Till he by miracle was approven King:
And that his grave should be a mystery
From all men, like his birth; and could he find
A woman in her womanhood as great

283-295. See "The Coming of Arthur," ll. 365-400, note.
288. **Bude and Bos,** districts of the same part of England as
Lyonesse.
291. **Tintagil,** see "The Coming of Arthur," l. 186, note.

As he was in his manhood, then, he sang,
The twain together well might change the world.
But even in the middle of his song
₄₀₀ He falter'd, and his hand fell from the harp,
And pale he turn'd, and reel'd, and would have fall'n,
But that they stay'd him up; nor would he tell
His vision; but what doubt that he foresaw
This evil work of Lancelot and the Queen?"

₄₀₅    Then thought the Queen, "Lo! they have set
        her on,
Our simple-seeming Abbess and her nuns,
To play upon me," and bow'd her head nor spake.
Whereat the novice crying, with clasp'd hands,
Shame on her own garrulity garrulously,
₄₁₀ Said the good nuns would check her gadding
        tongue
Full often, "and, sweet lady, if I seem
To vex an ear too sad to listen to me,
Unmannerly, with prattling and the tales
Which my good father told me, check me too,
₄₁₅ Nor let me shame my father's memory, one
Of noblest manners, tho' himself would say
Sir Lancelot had the noblest; and he died,
Kill'd in a tilt, come next, five summers back,
And left me; but of others who remain,
₄₂₀ And of the two first-famed for courtesy —
And pray you check me if I ask amiss —
But pray you, which had noblest, while you moved
Among them, Lancelot, or our lord the King?"

    Then the pale Queen look'd up and answer'd her,
₄₂₅ "Sir Lancelot, as became a noble knight,
Was gracious to all ladies, and the same

In open battle or the tilting-field
Forbore his own advantage, and the King
In open battle or the tilting-field
330 Forbore his own advantage, and these two
Were the most nobly-manner'd men of all;
For manners are not idle, but the fruit
Of loyal nature, and of noble mind."

"Yea," said the maid, "be manners such fair
fruit?
335 Then Lancelot's needs must be a thousand-fold
Less noble, being, as all rumor runs,
The most disloyal friend in all the world."

To which a mournful answer made the Queen:
"O closed about by narrowing nunnery-walls,
340 What knowest thou of the world, and all its lights
And shadows, all the wealth and all the woe?
If ever Lancelot, that most noble knight,
Were for one hour less noble than himself,
Pray for him that he scape the doom of fire,
345 And weep for her who drew him to his doom."

"Yea," said the little novice, "I pray for both;
But I should all as soon believe that his,
Sir Lancelot's, were as noble as the King's,
As I could think, sweet lady, yours would be
350 Such as they are, were you the sinful Queen."

So she, like many another babbler, hurt
Whom she would soothe, and harm'd where she
would heal;
For here a sudden flush of wrathful heat
Fired all the pale face of the Queen, who cried,

355 " Such as thou art be never maiden more
     For ever !  thou their tool, set on to plague
     And play upon, and harry me, petty spy
     And traitress."   When that storm of anger brake
     From Guinevere, aghast the maiden rose,
360 White as her veil, and stood before the Queen
     As tremulously as foam upon the beach
     Stands in a wind, ready to break and fly,
     And when the Queen had added, " Get thee hence,"
     Fled frighted.   Then that other left alone
365 Sigh'd, and began to gather heart again,
     Saying in herself, " The simple, fearful child
     Meant nothing, but my own too-fearful guilt,
     Simpler than any child, betrays itself.
     But help me, heaven, for surely I repent.
370 For what is true repentance but in thought —
     Not ev'n in inmost thought to think again
     The sins that made the past so pleasant to us :
     And I have sworn never to see him more,
     To see him more."

                         And ev'n in saying this,
375 Her memory from old habit of the mind
     Went slipping back upon the golden days
     In which she saw him first, when Lancelot came,
     Reputed the best knight and goodliest man,
     Ambassador, to lead her to his lord
380 Arthur, and led her forth, and far ahead
     Of his and her retinue moving, they,
     Rapt in sweet talk or lively, all on love
     And sport and tilts and pleasure (for the time
     Was maytime, and as yet no sin was dream'd),
385 Rode under groves that look'd a paradise

                 366. Fearful = frightened.

Of blossom, over sheets of hyacinth
That seem'd the heavens upbreaking thro' the earth,
And on from hill to hill, and every day
Beheld at noon in some delicious dale
390 The silk pavilions of King Arthur raised
For brief repast or afternoon repose
By couriers gone before; and on again,
Till yet once more ere set of sun they saw
The Dragon of the great Pendragonship,
395 That crown'd the state pavilion of the King,
Blaze by the rushing brook or silent well.

But when the Queen immersed in such a trance,
And moving thro' the past unconsciously,
Came to that point where first she saw the King
400 Ride toward her from the city, sigh'd to find
Her journey done, glanced at him, thought him cold,
High, self-contain'd, and passionless, not like him,
" Not like my Lancelot "— while she brooded thus
And grew half-guilty in her thoughts again,
405 There rode an armed warrior to the doors.
A murmuring whisper thro' the nunnery ran,
Then on a sudden a cry, " The King ! "   She sat
Stiff-stricken, listening ; but when armed feet
Thro' the long gallery from the outer doors
410 Rang coming, prone from off her seat she fell,
And grovell'd with her face against the floor :
There with her milkwhite arms and shadowy hair
She made her face a darkness from the King :
And in the darkness heard his armed feet
415 Pause by her ; then came silence, then a voice,

394. **The Dragon of the great Pendragonship**; for the use
of the dragon as Arthur's emblem see " Lancelot and Elaine.'
ll. 431–440.   For Pendragon see *ibid.* l. 422, note.

Monotonous and hollow like a ghost's
Denouncing judgment, but, tho' changed, **the**
 King's :

   " Liest thou here so low, the child of one
I honor'd, happy, dead before thy shame ?
120 Well is it that no child is born of thee.
The children born of thee are sword and fire,
Red ruin, and the breaking up of laws,
The craft of kindred and the godless hosts
Of heathen swarming o'er the Northern Sea ;
425 Whom I, while yet Sir Lancelot, my right arm,
The mightiest of my knights, abode with me,
Have everywhere about this land of Christ
In twelve great battles ruining overthrown.
And knowest thou now from whence I come — from
 him,
430 From waging bitter war with him : and he,
That did not shun to smite me in worse way,
Had yet that grace of courtesy in him left,
He spared to lift his hand against the King
Who made him knight : but many a knight **was**
 slain ;
435 And many more, and all his kith and kin
Clave to him, and abode in his own land.
And many more when Modred raised revolt,
Forgetful of their troth and fealty, clave
To Modred, and a remnant stays with me.
440 And of this remnant will I leave a part,
True men who love me still, for whom I live,
To guard thee in the wild hour coming on,
Lest but a hair of this low head be harm'd.

   428. **Twelve great battles**; see "Lancelot and Elaine," **ll**
286–300, note.

Fear not: thou shalt be guarded till my death.
145 Howbeit I know, if ancient prophecies
Have err'd not, that I march to meet my doom.
Thou hast not made my life so sweet to me,
That I the King should greatly care to live;
For thou hast spoilt the purpose of my life.
150 Bear with me for the last time while I show,
Ev'n for thy sake, the sin which thou hast sinn'd.
For when the Roman left us, and their law
Relax'd its hold upon us, and the ways
Were fill'd with rapine, here and there a deed
155 Of prowess done redress'd a random wrong.
But I was first of all the kings who drew
The knighthood-errant of this realm and all
The realms together under me, their Head,
In that fair Order of my Table Round,
160 A glorious company, the flower of men,
To serve as model for the mighty world,
And be the fair beginning of a time.
I made them lay their hands in mine and swear
To reverence the King, as if he were
165 Their conscience, and their conscience as their King,
To break the heathen and uphold the Christ,
To ride abroad redressing human wrongs,
To speak no slander, no, nor listen to it,
To honor his own word as if his God's,
170 To lead sweet lives in purest chastity,
To love one maiden only, cleave to her,
And worship her by years of noble deeds,
Until they won her; for indeed I knew
Of no more subtle master under heaven
175 Than is the maiden passion for a maid,
Not only to keep down the base in man,
But teach high thought, and amiable words

And courtliness, and the desire of fame,
And love of truth, and all that makes a man.
180 And all this throve before I wedded thee,
Believing, 'Lo mine helpmate, one to feel
My purpose and rejoicing in my joy.'
Then came thy shameful sin with Lancelot;
Then came the sin of Tristram and Isolt;
185 Then others, following these my mightiest knights
And drawing foul ensample from fair names,
Sinn'd also, till the loathsome opposite
Of all my heart had destined did obtain,
And all thro' thee! so that this life of mine
190 I guard as God's high gift from scathe and wrong,
Not greatly care to lose; but rather think
Had sad it were for Arthur, should he live,
To sit once more within his lonely hall,
And miss the wonted number of my knights,
195 And miss to hear high talk of noble deeds
As in the golden days before thy sin.
For which of us, who might be left, could speak
Of the pure heart, nor seem to glance at thee?
And in thy bowers of Camelot or of Usk
500 Thy shadow still would glide from room to room,
And I should evermore be vext with thee
In hanging robe or vacant ornament,
Or ghostly footfall echoing on the stair.
For think not, tho' thou wouldst not love thy
    lord,
505 Thy lord has wholly lost his love for thee.
I am not made of so slight elements.

484. **Tristram and Isolt**; their story is told in "The Last Tournament," the Idyll next before "Guinevere."
499. **Usk**; Caerleon-upon-Usk, still a town near the southeastern boundary of Wales, was one of Arthur's seats.

Yet must I leave thee, woman, to thy shame.
I hold that man the worst of public foes
  Who either for his own or children's sake,
510 To save his blood from scandal, lets the wife
Whom he knows false, abide and rule the house:
For being thro' his cowardice allow'd
Her station, taken everywhere for pure,
She like a new disease, unknown to men,
15 Creeps, no precaution used, among the crowd,
Makes wicked lightnings of her eyes, and saps
The fealty of our friends, and stirs the pulse
With devil's leaps, and poisons half the young.
Worst of the worst were that man he that reigns!
20 Better the King's waste hearth and aching heart
Than thou reseated in thy place of light,
The mockery of my people, and their bane."

    He paused, and in the pause she crept an inch
Nearer, and laid her hands about his feet.
525 Far off a solitary trumpet blew.
Then waiting by the doors the warhorse neigh'd
As at a friend's voice, and he spake again:

    "Yet think not that I come to urge thy crimes,
I did not come to curse thee, Guinevere,
530 I, whose vast pity almost makes me die
To see thee, laying there thy golden head,
My pride in happier summers, at my feet.
The wrath which forced my thoughts on that fierce
    law,
The doom of treason and the flaming death,
535 (When first I learnt thee hidden here) is past.

534. **The flaming death**, at the stake, from which Lancelot,
in Malory, saved her.

The pang — which while I weigh'd thy heart with
        one
Too wholly true to dream untruth in thee,
Made my tears burn — is also past, in part.
And all is past, the sin is sinn'd, and I,
540 Lo! I forgive thee, as Eternal God
Forgives: do thou for thine own soul the rest.
But how to take last leave of all I loved?
O golden hair, with which I used to play
Not knowing!   O imperial-moulded form,
545 And beauty such as never woman wore,
Until it came a kingdom's curse with thee —
I cannot touch thy lips, they are not mine,
But Lancelot's: nay, they never were the King's.
I cannot take thy hand; that too is flesh,
550 And in the flesh thou hast sinn'd; ~~and mine own
        flesh,~~
~~Here looking down on thine polluted, cries~~
'~~I loathe thee:~~' yet not less, O Guinevere,
~~For I was ever virgin save for thee,~~
My love thro' flesh hath wrought into my life
555 So far, that my doom is, I love thee still.
Let no man dream but that I love thee still.
Perchance, and so thou purify thy soul,
And so thou lean on our fair father Christ,
Hereafter in that world where all are pure
560 We too may meet before high God, and thou
Wilt spring to me, and claim me thine, and know
I am thine husband — not a smaller soul,
Nor Lancelot, nor another.   Leave me that,
I charge thee, my last hope.   Now must I hence.
565 Thro' the thick night I hear the trumpet blow:
They summon me their King to lead mine hosts
Far down to that great battle in the west,

Where I must strike against the man they call
My sister's son — no kin of mine, who leagues
570 With Lords of the White Horse, heathen, and
    knights,
Traitors — and strike him dead, and meet myself
Death, or I know not what mysterious doom.
And thou remaining here wilt learn the event;
But hither shall I never come again,
575 Never lie by thy side; see thee no more —
Farewell!"

          And while she grovell'd at his feet,
She felt the King's breath wander o'er her neck,
And in the darkness o'er her fallen head,
Perceived the waving of his hands that blest.

580    Then, listening till those armed steps were gone,
Rose the pale Queen, and in her anguish found
The casement: "peradventure," so she thought,
"If I might see his face, and not be seen."
And lo, he sat on horseback at the door!
585 And near him the sad nuns with each a light
Stood, and he gave them charge about the Queen,
To guard and foster her for evermore.
And while he spake to these his helm was lower'd,
To which for crest the golden dragon clung
590 Of Britain; so she did not see the face,
Which then was an angel's, but she saw,
Wet with the mists and smitten by the lights,
The Dragon of the great Pendragonship
Blaze, making all the night a steam of fire.
595 And even then he turn'd; and more and more
The moony vapor rolling round the King,

568, 569. The man they call My sister's son, Modred.

Who seem'd the phantom of a Giant in it,
Enwound him fold by fold, and made him gray
And grayer, till himself became as mist
600 Before her, moving ghostlike to his doom.

Then she stretch'd out her arms and cried aloud
"O Arthur!" there her voice brake suddenly,
Then — as a stream that spouting from a cliff
Fails in mid air, but gathering at the base
605 Re-makes itself, and flashes down the vale —
Went on in passionate utterance:

"Gone — my lord!
Gone thro' my sin to slay and to be slain!
And he forgave me, and I could not speak.
Farewell? I should have answer'd his farewell.
610 His mercy choked me. Gone, my lord the King,
My own true lord! how dare I call him mine?
The shadow of another cleaves to me,
And makes me one pollution: he, the King,
Call'd me polluted: shall I kill myself?
615 What help in that? I cannot kill my sin,
If soul be soul; nor can I kill my shame;
No, nor by living can I live it down.
The days will grow to weeks, the weeks to months,
The months will add themselves and make the years,
620 The years will roll into the centuries,
And mine will ever be a name of scorn.
I must not dwell on that defeat of fame.
Let the world be; that is but of the world
What else? what hope? I think there was a hope,
625 Except he mock'd me when he spake of hope;
His hope he call'd it; but he never mocks,
For mockery is the fume of little hearts.

And blessed be the King, who hath forgiven
  My wickedness to him, and let me hope
530 That in mine own heart I can live down sin
  And be his mate hereafter in the heavens
  Before high God.  Ah great and gentle lord,
  Who wast, as is the conscience of a saint
  Among his warring senses, to thy knights —
535 To whom my false voluptuous pride, that took
  Full easily all impressions from below,
  Would not look up, or half-despised the height
  To which I would not or I could not climb —
  I thought I could not breathe in that fine air,
540 That pure severity of perfect light —
  I wanted warmth and color which I found
  In Lancelot — now I see thee what thou art,
  Thou art the highest and most human too,
  Not Lancelot, nor another.  Is there none
545 Will tell the King I love him tho' so late?
  Now — ere he goes to the great Battle? none:
  Myself must tell him in that purer life,
  But now it were too daring.  Ah my God,
  What might I not have made of thy fair world,
550 Had I but loved thy highest creature here?
  It was my duty to have loved the highest:
  It surely was my profit had I known:
  It would have been my pleasure had I seen.
  We needs must love the highest when we see it,
555 Not Lancelot, nor another."

                    Here her hand
Grasp'd, made her vail her eyes: she look'd and saw
The novice, weeping, suppliant, and said to her,

633, 634. **The conscience of a saint Among his warring
senses;** see Introductory Sketch, p. 5.

"Yea, little maid, for am not _I_ forgiven?"
Then glancing up beheld the holy nuns
660 All round her, weeping; and her heart was loosed
Within her, and she wept with these and said,

"Ye know me then, that wicked one who broke
The vast design and purpose of the King.
O shut me round with narrowing nunnery-walls,
665 Meek maidens, from the voices crying 'shame.'
I must not scorn myself: he loves me still.
Let no one dream but that he loves me still.
So let me, if you do not shudder at me
Nor shun to call me sister, dwell with you;
670 Wear black and white, and be a nun like you,
Fast with your fasts, not feasting with your feasts;
Grieve with your griefs, not grieving at your joys,
But not rejoicing; mingle with your rites;
Pray and be pray'd for; lie before your shrines;
675 Do each low office of your holy house;
Walk your dim cloister, and distribute dole
To poor sick people, richer in His eyes
Who ransom'd us, and haler too than I;
And treat their loathsome hurts and heal mine
          own;
680 And so wear out in almsdeed and in prayer
The sombre close of that voluptuous day,
Which wrought the ruin of my lord the King."

She said: they took her to themselves: and she,
Still hoping, fearing, "is it yet too late?"
685 Dwelt with them, till in time their Abbess died.
Then she, for her good deeds and her pure life,

676. **Dole** = alms.
678. **Haler** = sounder — inwardly.

And for the power of ministration in her,
And likewise for the high rank she had borne,
Was chosen Abbess, there, an Abbess, lived
For three brief years, and there, an Abbess, past
To where beyond these voices there is peace.

# THE PASSING OF ARTHUR.

THAT story which the bold Sir Bedivere,
First made and latest left of all the knights,
Told, when the man was no more than a voice
In the white winter of his age, to those
With whom he dwelt, new faces, other minds.

For on their march to westward, Bedivere,
Who slowly paced among the slumbering host,
Heard in his tent the moanings of the King:

"I found Him in the shining of the stars,
I mark'd Him in the flowering of His fields,
But in His ways with men I find Him not.
I waged His wars, and now I pass and die.
O me! for why is all around us here
As if some lesser god had made the world,
But had not force to shape it as he would,
Till the High God behold it from beyond,

The Passing of Arthur, as we have already said in the
Introductory Sketch, is identical with the greater portion of the
"Morte d'Arthur" of 1842, and in its present form first ap-
peared as one of the Idylls in the volume of 1869. The passage
in Malory from which its most important part is taken may also
be found in the Introductory Sketch, and is well worth reading
in direct connection with the poem.

2. **First made**; see "The Coming of Arthur," l. 173.

And enter it, and make it beautiful?
Or else as if the world were wholly fair,
But that these eyes of men are dense and dim,
20 And have not power to see it as it is:
Perchance, because we see not to the close;—
For I, being simple, thought to work His will,
And have but stricken with the sword in vain;
And all whereon I lean'd in wife and friend
25 Is traitor to my peace, and all my realm
Reels back into the beast, and is no more.
My God, thou hast forgotten me in my death:
Nay — God my Christ — I pass but shall not die."

    Then, ere that last weird battle in the west,
30 There came on Arthur sleeping, Gawain kill'd
In Lancelot's war, the ghost of Gawain blown
Along a wandering wind, and past his ear
Went shrilling, "Hollow, hollow all delight!
Hail, King! to-morrow thou shalt pass away.
35 Farewell! there is an isle of rest for thee.
And I am blown along a wandering wind,
And hollow, hollow, hollow all delight."
And fainter onward, like wild birds that change
Their season in the night and wail their way
40 From cloud to cloud, down the long wind the dream
Shrill'd; but in going mingled with dim cries
Far in the moonlit haze among the hills,
As of some lonely city sack'd by night,
When all is lost, and wife and child with wail
45 Pass to new lords! and Arthur woke and call'd,

28. **I pass but shall not die** ; the old belief expressed in
other Idylls. See "The Coming of Arthur," ll. 420, 421, note.

31. **The ghost of Gawain** ; in Malory, too, the king received
such a warning as Gawain here gives.

"Who spake? A dream. O light upon the wind,
Thine, Gawain, was the voice — are these dim cries
Thine? or doth all that haunts the waste and wild
Mourn, knowing it will go along with me?"

50 This heard the bold Sir Bedivere and spake:
"O me, my King, let pass whatever will,
Elves, and the harmless glamour of the field;
But in their stead thy name and glory cling
To all high places like a golden cloud
55 For ever: but as yet thou shalt not pass.
Light was Gawain in life, and light in death
Is Gawain, for the ghost is as the man;
And care not thou for dreams from him, but rise —
I hear the steps of Modred in the west,
60 And with him many of thy people, and knights
Once thine, whom thou hast loved, but grosser grown
Than heathen, spitting at their vows and thee.
Right well in heart they know thee for the King.
Arise, go forth and conquer as of old."

65 Then spake King Arthur to Sir Bedivere:
"Far other is this battle in the west
Whereto we move, than when we strove in youth,
And brake the petty kings, and fought with Rome,
Or thrust the heathen from the Roman wall,
70 And shook him thro' the north. Ill doom is mine
To war against my people and my knights.
The king who fights his people fights himself.
And they my knights, who loved me once, the
    stroke
That strikes them dead is as my death to me.

**56. Light was Gawain in life**; one side of his character was
shown in "Lancelot and Elaine." See especially l. 557.

75 Yet let us hence, and find or feel a way
   Thro' this blind haze, which ever since I saw
   One lying in the dust at Almesbury,
   Hath folded in the passes of the world."


   Then rose the King and moved his host by night,
80 And ever push'd Sir Modred, league by league,
   Back to the sunset bound of Lyonnesse —
   A land of old upheaven from the abyss
   By fire, to sink into the abyss again;
   Where fragments of forgotten peoples dwelt,
85 And the long mountains ended in a coast
   Of ever-shifting sand, and far away
   The phantom circle of a moaning sea.
   There the pursuer could pursue no more,
   And he that fled no further fly the King;
90 And there, that day when the great light of heaven
   Burn'd at his lowest in the rolling year,
   On the waste sand by the waste sea they closed.
   Nor ever yet had Arthur fought a fight
   Like this last dim, weird battle of the west.
95 A deathwhite mist slept over sand and sea:
   Whereof the chill, to him who breathed it, drew
   Down with his blood, till all his heart was cold
   With formless fear; and ev'n on Arthur fell
   Confusion, since he saw not whom he fought,
100 For friend and foe were shadows in the mist,
   And friend slew friend not knowing whom he slew;
   And some had visions out of golden youth,
   And some beheld the faces of old ghosts
   Look in upon the battle; and in the mist

   83. **To sink into the abyss again**; a reference to the belief
that Lyonesse, between Cornwall and the Scilly Islands, is now
submerged.

105 Was many a noble deed, many a base,
And chance and craft and strength in single fights,
And ever and anon with host to host
Shocks, and the splintering spear, the hard mail
    hewn,
Shield-breakings, and the clash of brands, the crash
110 Of battleaxes on shatter'd helms, and shrieks
After the Christ, of those who falling down
Look'd up for heaven, and only saw the mist;
And shouts of heathen and the traitor knights,
Oaths, insult, filth, and monstrous blasphemies,
115 Sweat, writhings, anguish, laboring of the lungs
In that close mist, and cryings for the light,
Moans of the dying, and voices of the dead.

Last, as by some one deathbed after wail
Of suffering, silence follows, or thro' death
120 Or deathlike swoon, thus over all that shore,
Save for some whisper of the seething seas,
A dead hush fell; but when the dolorous day
Grew drearier toward twilight falling, came
A bitter wind, clear from the North, and blew
125 The mist aside, and with that wind the tide
Rose, and the pale King glanced across the field
Of battle: but no man was moving there;
Nor any cry of Christian heard thereon,
Nor yet of heathen; only the wan wave
130 Brake in among dead faces, to and fro
Swaying the helpless hands, and up and down
Tumbling the hollow helmets of the fallen,
And shiver'd brands that once had fought with
    Rome,
And rolling far along the gloomy shores
135 The voice of days of old and days to be.

Then spake King Arthur to Sir Bedivere,
And whiter than the mist that all day long
Had held the field of battle was the King:

"Hearest thou this great voice that shakes the
world
140 And wastes the narrow realm whereon we move,
And beats upon the faces of the dead,
My dead, as tho' they had not died for me?—
O Bedivere, for on my heart hath fall'n
Confusion, till I know not what I am,
145 Nor whence I am, nor whether I be King.
Behold, I seem but King among the dead."

Then spake the bold Sir Bedivere: "My King,
King everywhere! and so the dead have kings,
There also will I worship thee as King.
150 Yet still thy life is whole, and still I live
Who love thee; but who hates thee, he that brought
The heathen back among us, yonder stands,
Modred, unharm'd, the traitor of thine house."

Then spake the King: "My house had been my
doom,
155 But call not thou this traitor of my house
Who hath but dwelt beneath one roof with me.
My house are rather they who sware my vows,
Yea, even while they brake them, own'd me King.
And well for thee, saying in my dark hour,
160 When all the purport of my throne hath fail'd,
That quick or dead thou holdest me for King.
King am I, whatsoever be their cry;
And one last act of kinghood shalt thou see

148. **So**, in the best familiar sense of *provided that, if.*

Yet, ere I pass." And uttering this the King
165 Made at the man : then Modred smote his liege
Hard on that helm which many a heathen sword
Had beaten thin ; while Arthur at one blow,
Striking the last stroke with Excalibur,
Slew him, and all but slain himself, he fell.

170 So all day long the noise of battle roll'd
Among the mountains by the winter sea ;
Until King Arthur's Table, man by man,
Had fall'n in Lyonnesse about their lord,
King Arthur. Then, because his wound was
     deep,
175 The bold Sir Bedivere uplifted him,
And bore him to a chapel nigh the field,
A broken chancel with a broken cross,
That stood on a dark strait of barren land :
On one side lay the Ocean, and on one
180 Lay a great water, and the moon was full.

Then spake King Arthur to Sir Bedivere :
" The sequel of to-day unsolders all
The goodliest fellowship of famous knights
Whereof this world holds record. Such a sleep
185 They sleep — the men I loved. I think that we
Shall never more, at any future time,
Delight our souls with talk of knightly deeds,
Walking about the gardens and the halls
Of Camelot, as in the days that were.
190 I perish by this people which I made, —
Tho' Merlin sware that I should come again

168. **Excalibur** ; see "The Coming of Arthur," l. 285, note.
170. With this line, following the introduction called " The
Epic," Tennyson's early poem the " Morte d'Arthur " began.

To rule once more; but, let what will be, be,
I am so deeply smitten thro' the helm
That without help I cannot last till morn.
195 Thou therefore take my brand Excalibur,
Which was my pride: for thou rememberest how
In those old days, one summer noon, an arm
Rose up from out the bosom of the lake,
Clothed in white samite, mystic, wonderful,
200 Holding the sword — and how I row'd across
And took it, and have worn it, like a king;
And, wheresoever I am sung or told
In aftertime, this also shall be known:
But now delay not: take Excalibur,
205 And fling him far into the middle mere:
Watch what thou seëst, and lightly bring me word.'

To him replied the bold Sir Bedivere:
"It is not meet, Sir King, to leave thee thus,
Aidless, alone, and smitten thro' the helm —
210 A little thing may harm a wounded man:
Yet I thy hest will all perform at full,
Watch what I see, and lightly bring thee word."

So saying, from the ruin'd shrine he stept,
And in the moon athwart the place of tombs,
215 Where lay the mighty bones of ancient men,
Old knights, and over them the sea-wind sang
Shrill, chill, with flakes of foam.     He, stepping
down

195. It is from this point that the narrative of Malory is
most closely followed.
197. **An arm Rose up**; as related in Malory, i., xxiii.
205. **Him**, as if Arthur thought of the sword as a personal
comrade.

By zigzag paths, and juts of pointed rock,
Came on the shining levels of the lake.


'20   There drew he forth the brand Excalibur,
And o'er him, drawing it, the winter moon,
Brightening the skirts of a long cloud, ran forth
And sparkled keen with frost against the hilt:
For all the haft twinkled with diamond sparks,
'25 Myriads of topaz-lights, and jacinth-work
Of subtlest jewellery.  He gazed so long
That both his eyes were dazzled as he stood,
This way and that dividing the swift mind,
In act to throw: but at the last it seem'd
'30 Better to leave Excalibur conceal'd
There in the many-knotted waterflags,
That whistled stiff and dry about the marge.
So strode he back slow to the wounded King


  Then spake King Arthur to Sir Bedivere:
235 "Hast thou perform'd my mission which I gave?
What is it thou hast seen? or what hast heard?"


  And answer made the bold Sir Bedivere:
"I heard the ripple washing in the reeds,
And the wild water lapping on the crag."


240   To whom replied King Arthur, faint and pale:
"Thou hast betray'd thy nature and thy name,
Not rendering true answer, as beseem'd
Thy fëalty, nor like a noble knight:
For surer sign had follow'd, either hand,
245 Or voice, or else a motion of the mere.

**241. Thy name**; this may be taken for *fame* or *reputation*, as before in the Idylls, or possibly as referring to the *-vere* of his name, meaning *true*.

This is a shameful thing for men to lie.
Yet now, I charge thee, quickly go again,
As thou art lief and dear, and do the thing
I bade thee, watch, and lightly bring me word.'

250    Then went Sir Bedivere the second time
Across the ridge, and paced beside the mere,
Counting the dewy pebbles, fix'd in thought ;
But when he saw the wonder of the hilt,
How curiously and strangely chased, he smote
255 His palms together, and he cried aloud :

"And if indeed I cast the brand away,
Surely a precious thing, one worthy note,
Should thus be lost for ever from the earth,
Which might have pleased the eyes of many men
260 What good should follow this, if this were done ?
What harm, undone ?   Deep harm to disobey,
Seeing obedience is the bond of rule.
Were it well to obey then, if a king demand
An act unprofitable, against himself ?
265 The King is sick, and knows not what he does.
What record, or what relic of my lord
Should be to aftertime, but empty breath
And rumors of a doubt ?   But were this kept,
Stored in some treasure-house of mighty kings,
270 Some one might show it at a joust of arms,
Saying, ' King Arthur's sword, Excalibur,
Wrought by the lonely maiden of the Lake.
Nine years she wrought it, sitting in the deeps
Upon the hidden bases of the hills.'
275 So might some old man speak in the aftertime
To all the people, winning reverence.
But now much honor and much fame were lost."

So spake he, clouded with his own conceit,
And hid Excalibur the second time,
280 And so strode back slow to the wounded King.

Then spoke King Arthur, breathing heavily:
"What is it thou hast seen? or what hast heard?"

And answer made the bold Sir Bedivere:
"I heard the water lapping on the crag,
285 And the long ripple washing in the reeds."

To whom replied King Arthur, much in wrath:
"Ah, miserable and unkind, untrue,
Unknightly, traitor-hearted! Woe is me!
Authority forgets a dying king,
290 Laid widow'd of the power in his eye
That bow'd the will. I see thee what thou art,
For thou, the latest-left of all my knights,
In whom should meet the offices of all,
Thou wouldst betray me for the precious hilt ;
295 Either from lust of gold, or like a girl
Valuing the giddy pleasure of the eyes.
Yet, for a man may fail in duty twice,
And the third time may prosper, get thee hence :
But, if thou spare to fling Excalibur,
300 I will arise and slay thee with my hands."

Then quickly rose Sir Bedivere, and ran,
And, leaping down the ridges lightly, plunged
Among the bulrush beds, and clutch'd the sword,
And strongly wheel'd and threw it. The great
brand
105 Made lightnings in the splendor of the moon,

297. **For,** since.

And flashing round and round, and whirl'd in an
    arch,
Shot like a streamer of the northern morn,
Seen where the moving isles of winter shock
By night, with noises of the Northern Sea.
310 So flash'd and fell the brand Excalibur:
But ere he dipt the surface, rose an arm
Clothed in white samite, mystic, wonderful,
And caught him by the hilt, and brandish'd him
Three times, and drew him under in the mere.
315 And lightly went the other to the King.


    Then spoke King Arthur, drawing thicker breath :
" Now see I by thine eyes that this is done.
Speak out : what is it thou hast heard, or seen ? "


    And answer made the bold Sir Bedivere :
320 " Sir King, I closed mine eyelids, lest the gems
Should blind my purpose, for I never saw,
Nor shall see, here or elsewhere, till I die,
Not tho' I live three lives of mortal men,
So great a miracle as yonder hilt.
325 Then with both hands I flung him, wheeling him ;
But when I look'd again, behold an arm,
Clothed in white samite, mystic, wonderful,
That caught him by the hilt and brandish'd him
Three times, and drew him under in the mere."


    306. **Whirl'd in an arch ;** *in* and *an* must almost be con-
tracted in reading into one syllable.   The line, like many others
in the Idylls, departs from structural exactness, in order to
make an effect in sound corresponding with the sense.

    307. **The northern morn** = *the aurora borealis.*

    308. **Where the moving isles of winter,** etc. = where the
floes of ice crash together by night in the Northern Sea.

430    And answer made King Arthur, breathing hard:
" My end draws nigh; 't is time that I were gone.
Make broad thy shoulders to receive my weight,
And bear me to the margin; yet I fear
My wound hath taken cold, and I shall die."

335    So saying, from the pavement he half rose,
Slowly, with pain, reclining on his arm,
And looking wistfully with wide blue eyes
As in a picture.   Him Sir Bedivere
Remorsefully regarded thro' his tears,
40 And would have spoken, but he found not words;
Then took with care, and kneeling on one knee,
O'er both his shoulders drew the languid hands,
And rising bore him thro' the place of tombs.

   But, as he walk'd, King Arthur panted hard,
345 Like one that feels a nightmare on his bed
When all the house is mute.   So sigh'd the King,
Muttering and murmuring at his ear, " Quick,
    quick!
I fear it is too late, and I shall die."
But the other swiftly strode from ridge to ridge,
350 Clothed with his breath, and looking, as he walk'd,
Larger than human on the frozen hills.
He heard the deep behind him, and a cry
Before.   His own thought drove him like a goad.
Dry clash'd his harness in the icy caves
355 And barren chasms, and all to left and right
The bare black cliff clang'd round him, as he based
His feet on juts of slippery crag that rang
Sharp-smitten with the dint of armed heels —
And on a sudden, lo! the level lake,
460 And the long glories of the winter moon.
        350, 351. See " Guinevere," ll. 596–604.

Then saw they how there hove a dusky barge,
Dark as a funeral scarf from stem to stern,
Beneath them ; and descending they were ware
That all the decks were dense with stately forms,
365 Black-stoled, black-hooded, like a dream — by these
Three Queens with crowns of gold : and from them
 rose
A cry that shiver'd to the tingling stars,
And, as it were one voice, an agony
Of lamentation, like a wind that shrills
370 All night in a waste land, where no one comes,
Or hath come, since the making of the world.

Then murmur'd Arthur, " Place me in the barge."
So to the barge they came. There those three
 Queens
Put forth their hands, and took the King, and
 wept.
375 But she, that rose the tallest of them all
And fairest, laid his head upon her lap,
And loosed the shatter'd casque, and chafed his
 hands,
And call'd him by his name, complaining loud,
And dropping bitter tears against a brow
380 Striped with dark blood : for all his face was white
And colorless, and like the wither'd moon
Smote by the fresh beam of the springing east ;
And all his greaves and cuisses dash'd with drops
Of onset ; and the light and lustrous curls —
385 That made his forehead like a rising sun
High from the daïs-throne — were parch'd with
 dust ;
Or, clotted into points and hanging loose,
Mix'd with the knightly growth that fringed his lips.

So like a shatter'd column lay the King;
Not like that Arthur who, with lance in rest,
From spur to plume a star of tournament,
Shot thro' the lists at Camelot, and charged
Before the eyes of ladies and of kings.

    Then loudly cried the bold Sir Bedivere:
"Ah! my Lord Arthur, whither shall I go?
Where shall I hide my forehead and my eyes?
For now I see the true old times are dead,
When every morning brought a noble chance,
And every chance brought out a noble knight.
Such times have been not since the light that led
The holy Elders with the gift of myrrh.
But now the whole Round Table is dissolved
Which was an image of the mighty world
And I, the last, go forth companionless,
And the days darken round me, and the years,
Among new men, strange faces, other minds."

    And slowly answer'd Arthur from the barge:
"The old order changeth, yielding place to new,
And God fulfils himself in many ways,
Lest one good custom should corrupt the world.
Comfort thyself: what comfort is in me?
I have lived my life, and that which I have done
May He within himself make pure! but thou,
If thou shouldst never see my face again,
Pray for my soul. More things are wrought by prayer
Than this world dreams of. Wherefore, let thy voice
Rise like a fountain for me night and day.

      408. See "The Coming of Arthur," l. 508.

For what are men better than sheep or goats
That nourish a blind life within the brain,
420 If, knowing God, they lift not hands of prayer
Both for themselves and those who call the
    friend?
For so the whole round earth is every way
Bound by gold chains about the feet of God.
But now farewell.   I am going a long way
425 With these thou seëst — if indeed I go
(For all my mind is clouded with a doubt) —
To the island-valley of Avilion;
Where falls not hail, or rain, or any snow,
Nor ever wind blows loudly; but it lies
430 Deep-meadow'd, happy, fair with orchard lawns
And bowery hollows crown'd with summer sea,
Where I will heal me of my grievous wound."

So said he, and the barge with oar and sail
Moved from the brink, like some full-breasted swa
435 That, fluting a wild carol ere her death,
Ruffles her pure cold plume, and takes the flood
With swarthy webs.   Long stood Sir Bedivere
Revolving many memories, till the hull
Look'd one black dot against the verge of dawn,
440 And on the mere the wailing died away.

But when that moan had past for evermore,
The stillness of the dead world's winter dawn
Amazed him, and he groan'd, "The King is gone.'
And therewithal came on him the weird rhyme,
445 "From the great deep to the great deep he goes."

434. **Like some full-breasted swan**; referring to th
familiar, if unscientific, belief that swans sing before they die.
440. With this line the " Morte d' Arthur " ended.
445. See "The Coming of Arthur," l. 410.

Whereat he slowly turn'd and slowly clomb
The last hard footstep of that iron crag ;
Thence mark'd the black hull moving yet, and cried,
" He passes to be King among the dead,
50 And after healing of his grievous wound
He comes again ; but — if he come no more —
O me, be yon dark Queens in yon black boat,
Who shriek'd and wail'd, the three whereat we
    gazed
On that high day, when, clothed with living light,
455 They stood before his throne in silence, friends
Of Arthur, who should help him at his need ? "

Then from the dawn it seem'd there came, but
    faint,
As from beyond the limit of the world,
Like the last echo born of a great cry,
460 Sounds, as if some fair city were one voice
Around a king returning from his wars.

Thereat once more he moved about, and clomb
Ev'n to the highest he could climb, and saw,
Straining his eyes beneath an arch of hand,
465 Or thought he saw, the speck that bare the King,
Down that long water opening on the deep
Somewhere far off, pass on and on, and go
From less to less and vanish into light.
And the new sun rose bringing the new year.

453. **The three whereat we gazed** : see " The Coming of
Arthur," ll. 275–278.

# ENGLISH LITERATURE

A Short History of England's Literature. By Eva March Tappan.

A Student's History of English Literature. By William Edward Simonds.

Lives of Great English Writers. From Chaucer to Browning. By W. S. Hinchman and Francis B. Gummere.

Masterpieces of British Literature. Edited by Horace E. Scudder.

Readings in English Prose of the 18th Century. Edited by Raymond Macdonald Alden.

A Victorian Anthology. Edited by Edmund Clarence Stedman.

# AMERICAN LITERATURE

A Short History of England's and America's Literature. By Eva March Tappan.

A Short History of America's Literature. With Selections from Colonial and Revolutionary Writers. By Eva March Tappan.

A History of American Literature. By William E. Simonds.

Masterpieces of American Literature. Edited by Horace E. Scudder.

Readings in English Prose of the 19th Century. Edited by Raymond Macdonald Alden. *Part I, Part II. Complete.*

The Chief American Prose Writers. Edited by Norman Foerster.

An American Anthology. Edited by Edmund Clarence Stedman. *Students' Edition.*

The Chief American Poets. Edited by Curtis Hidden Page.

The Little Book of Modern Verse. Edited by Jessie B. Rittenhouse. R.L.S. No. 254. *Library binding.*

The Little Book of American Poets. Edited by Jessie B. Rittenhouse. R.L.S. No. 255. *Library binding.*

A Treasury of War Poetry. Edited by George Herbert Clarke. R.L.S. No. 262. *Cloth.*

---

# HOUGHTON MIFFLIN COMPANY

1909

# LITERATURE SELECTIONS

**Short Stories of America.** Edited by ROBERT L. RAMSAY.

**Modern Prose and Poetry for Secondary Schools.** Edited by MARGARET ASHMUN.

**Prose Literature for Secondary Schools.** Edited by MARGARET ASHMUN.

**The High School Prize Speaker.** Edited by WILLIAM L. SNOW.

**American and English Classics for Grammar Grades.**

**Selections from the Riverside Literature Series for Fifth Grade Reading.**

**Selections from the Riverside Literature Series for Sixth Grade Reading.**

**Selections from the Riverside Literature Series for Seventh Grade Reading.**

**Selections from the Riverside Literature Series for Eighth Grade Reading.**

**American Classics.** (Poems and Prose.)

**American Poems.** Edited by HORACE E. SCUDDER.

**American Prose.** Edited by HORACE E. SCUDDER.

**Literary Masterpieces.**

**Masterpieces of American Literature.** Edited by HORACE E. SCUDDER.

**Masterpieces of British Literature.** Edited by HORACE E. SCUDDER.

**Masterpieces of Greek Literature.** (Translations.) Supervising editor, JOHN HENRY WRIGHT.

**Masterpieces of Latin Literature.** (Translations.) Edited by G. J. LAING.

---

## HOUGHTON MIFFLIN COMPANY

# THE CAMBRIDGE POETS — STUDENTS' EDITION

Robert Browning's Complete Poetical and Dramatic Works.
Burns's Complete Poetical Works.
Byron's Complete Poetical Works.
Dryden's Complete Poetical Works.
English and Scottish Ballads.
Keats's Complete Poetical Works and Letters.
Longfellow's Complete Poetical Works.
Milton's Complete Poetical Works.
Pope's Complete Poetical Works.
Shakespeare's Complete Works.
Shelley's Complete Poetical Works.
Spenser's Complete Poetical Works.
Tennyson's Poetical and Dramatic Works.
Whittier's Complete Poetical Works.
Wordsworth's Complete Poetical Works.

## ANTHOLOGIES: POETRY AND DRAMA

The Chief Middle English Poets. Translated and Edited by JESSIE L. WESTON.

The Chief British Poets of the Fourteenth and Fifteenth Centuries. Edited by W. A. NEILSON and K. G. T. WEBSTER.

The Leading English Poets from Chaucer to Browning. Edited by L. H. HOLT.

A Victorian Anthology. Edited by EDMUND CLARENCE STEDMAN.

The Chief American Poets. Edited by C. H. PAGE.

An American Anthology. Edited by EDMUND CLARENCE STEDMAN.

Little Book of Modern Verse. Edited by JESSIE B. RITTENHOUSE. R.L.S. No. 254.

Second Book of Modern Verse. Edited by JESSIE B. RITTENHOUSE. R.L.S. No. 267.

Little Book of American Poets. Edited by JESSIE B. RITTENHOUSE. R.L.S. No. 255.

High Tide. Edited by Mrs. WALDO RICHARDS. R.L.S. No. 256.

A Treasury of War Poetry. Edited by GEORGE H. CLARKE. R.L.S. No. 262.

The Chief Elizabethan Dramatists. Edited by W. A. NEILSON.

Chief European Dramatists. In Translation. Edited by BRANDER MATTHEWS.

Chief Contemporary Dramatists, First Series. Edited by THOMAS H. DICKINSON.

Chief Contemporary Dramatists, Second Series. Edited by THOMAS H. DICKINSON.

## HOUGHTON MIFFLIN COMPANY

# PLAYS OF SHAKESPEARE

**AS YOU LIKE IT.** No. 93. With Introductory and Explanatory Notes and Suggestions for Study.

**HAMLET.** No. 116. With an Introduction, Explanatory Notes, and Suggestions for Study by Helen Gray Cone, Professor of English in Hunter College.

**HENRY V.** No. 163. With an Introduction, a Bibliography, and Notes by Edward Everett Hale, Ph.D., Professor of English in Union College, Schenectady, N. Y.

**JULIUS CÆSAR.** No. 67. With an Introduction, Explanatory Notes, Suggestions for Study, and a Bibliography.

**KING LEAR.** No. 184. With an Introduction, Bibliography, and Explanatory Notes. Edited by Ashley H. Thorndike, Professor of English in Columbia University.

**MACBETH.** No. 106. With an Introduction, Explanatory Notes, and Suggestions for Special Study. With additional Notes by Helen Gray Cone.

**THE MERCHANT OF VENICE.** No. 55. With Introduction and Notes by Samuel Thurber, Late Master in the Girls' High School, Boston, Mass.

**A MIDSUMMER NIGHT'S DREAM.** No. 153. With an Introduction, Explanatory Notes, and an Appendix by Laura E. Lockwood, Ph.D., Associate Professor of English Language at Wellesley College.

**ROMEO AND JULIET.** No. 212. With Introduction and Notes by William Strunk, Jr., Professor of the English Language and Literature, Cornell University.

**THE TEMPEST.** No. 154. With an Introduction and Explanatory Notes. Edited by Edward Everett Hale, Ph.D.

**TWELFTH NIGHT.** No. 149. With an Introduction, Explanatory Notes, Suggestions for Special Study, and an Appendix. With additional Notes by Helen Gray Cone.

**SHAKESPEARE QUESTIONS.** No. 246. An Outline of the Study of Shakespeare's Plays, by Odell Shepard, Professor of English, Trinity College.

---

## HOUGHTON MIFFLIN COMPANY

1910

1882    **WHY WE CELEBRATE**    1922

The

# Fortieth Anniversary

of the

## Riverside Literature Series

### A force in the field of education

Two generations of pupils in our public schools and colleges have studied from the Riverside Literature Series, the oldest series of its kind and the first to offer to students the best of English and American literature in convenient and inexpensive form.

### The largest series of classics for school use

Here is a textbook library without equal for wealth and variety of material. It includes over 3300 literary masterpieces — history, biography, letters, essays, poetry, orations, fiction, drama, mythology. Over one third of the material included is not to be found in any similar series of classics.

### Represents the best scholarship in the country

Each volume in the series has received the most careful and scholarly editing available. Students of the Riverside Literature Series get the benefit of the very best teaching that the country can afford.

### Over a million copies sold yearly

Since 1882 the sales of the series have increased from 6000 copies to over a million copies a year. Wherever there are students of English or American literature, the Riverside Literature Series is in demand. Used in every State in the Union and in every dependency of the United States, it also finds its way into nearly a score of foreign countries.

## HOUGHTON MIFFLIN COMPANY

BOSTON    NEW YORK    CHICAGO    SAN FRANCISCO

2102

# NEW ISSUES IN THE
# Riverside Literature Series

## For the Grades

ALDRICH's **Marjorie Daw and Other Stories.** No. 265.

ANTIN's **At School in the Promised Land.** No. 245.

AUSTIN's **Standish of Standish, Dramatized.** No. 217.

BURROUGHS's **The Wit of a Duck, and Other Papers.** No. 259.

IRVING's **Tales from the Alhambra.** Adapted by Josephine Brower. No. 260.

**Kipling Stories and Poems Every Child Should Know.** Part I, No. 257. Part II, No. 258.

MUIR's **The Boyhood of a Naturalist.** No. 247.

SHARP's **Ways of the Woods.** No. 266.

WIGGIN's **Birds' Christmas Carol.** No. 232.

WIGGIN's **Rebecca of Sunnybrook Farm.** No. 264.

**Selections for Reading and Memorizing.** Grades I–VIII. Seven volumes, Nos. FF–MM inclusive.

## For High Schools

ARNOLD's **Essay on Wordsworth and Selected Lyrics by Wordsworth.** No. 269.

BOSWELL's **The Life of Johnson.** Abridged. No. 248.

BURROUGHS's **Nature Near Home, and Other Papers.** No. 270.

CLARKE's **A Treasury of War Poetry.** No. 262.

KELLER's **The Story of My Life.** No. 253.

**Liberty, Peace, and Justice.** (Documents and Addresses, 1776–1918.) No. 261.

MILLS's **Being Good to Bears.** No. 271.

PALMER's **Self-Cultivation in English.** No. 249.

PEABODY's **The Piper.** No. 263.

RICHARDS's **High Tide.** An Anthology. No. 256.

## For Colleges

DRINKWATER's **Abraham Lincoln.** A Play. No. 268.

HOWELLS's **A Modern Instance.** No. 252.

LOCKWOOD's **English Sonnets.** No. 244.

RITTENHOUSE's **The Little Book of American Poets.** No. 255.

RITTENHOUSE's **The Little Book of Modern Verse.** No. 254.

RITTENHOUSE's **Second Book of Modern Verse.** No. 267.

SHEPARD's **Shakespeare Questions.** No. 246.

SHERIDAN's **The School for Scandal.** No. 250.

**Sir Gawain and the Green Knight, and Piers the Ploughman.** No. 251.

---

## Houghton Mifflin Company
1940

# Riverside Literature Series

## LIBRARY BINDING

Sir Gawain and the Green Knight, and Piers the Ploughman. WEBSTER AND NEILSON.

Chaucer's The Prologue, The Knight's Tale, and The Nun's Priest's Tale. MATHER.

Ralph Roister Doister. CHILD.

The Second Shepherds' Play, Everyman, and Other Early Plays. CHILD.

Bacon's Essays. NORTHUP.

Shakespeare Questions. SHEPARD.

Milton's Of Education, Areopagitica, The Commonwealth. LOCKWOOD.

Boswell's Life of Johnson. JENSEN.

Goldsmith's The Good-Natured Man, and She Stoops to Conquer. DICKINSON.

Sheridan's The School for Scandal. WEBSTER.

Shelley's Poems. (Selected.) CLARKE.

Huxley's Autobiography, and Selected Essays. SNELL.

Selections from the Prose Works of Matthew Arnold. JOHNSON.

Selected Literary Essays from James Russell Lowell. HOWE and FOERSTER.

Howells's A Modern Instance.

Briggs's College Life.

Briggs's To College Girls.

Perry's The American Mind and American Idealism.

Burroughs's Studies in Nature and Literature.

Newman's University Subjects.

Bryce's Promoting Good Citizenship.

Eliot's The Training for an Effective Life.

English and American Sonnets. LOCKWOOD.

The Little Book of American Poets. RITTENHOUSE.

The Little Book of Modern Verse. RITTENHOUSE.

High Tide. An Anthology of Contemporary Poems. RICHARDS.

Minimum College Requirements in English for Study.

The Second Book of Modern Verse. RITTENHOUSE.

Abraham Lincoln. A Play. DRINKWATER.

# RIVERSIDE ESSAYS

Edited by ADA L. F. SNELL

*Associate Professor of English, Mount Holyoke College*

The purpose of the Riverside Essays is to present to students of English composition essays by modern authors which deal in a fresh way with such subjects as politics, science, literature, and nature. The close study of vigorous and artistic writing is generally acknowledged to be the best method of gaining a mastery of the technique of composition.

In the Riverside Essays the material consists of essays which, with few exceptions, have been printed entire. Other advantages of the Riverside Essays for both instructor and student lie in the fact that the material is presented in separate volumes, each of which is devoted to a single author and contains two or more representative essays.

Finally, the series has none of the earmarks of the ordinary textbook which the student passes on, marked and battered, to the next college generation. The books are attractively printed, and bound in the Library Binding of the Riverside Literature Series. The student will therefore be glad to keep these books for his own library.

## PROMOTING GOOD CITIZENSHIP
By JAMES BRYCE. With an Introduction. *Riverside Literature Series*, No. 227, Library Binding.

## STUDIES IN NATURE AND LITERATURE
By JOHN BURROUGHS. *Riverside Literature Series*, No. 226, Library Binding.

## UNIVERSITY SUBJECTS
By JOHN HENRY NEWMAN. *Riverside Literature Series*, No. 225, Library Binding.

## THE AMERICAN MIND AND AMERICAN IDEALISM
By BLISS PERRY. With an Introduction. *Riverside Literature Series*, No. 224, Library Binding.

---

## HOUGHTON MIFFLIN COMPANY

# Books on Patriotic Subjects

## I AM AN AMERICAN

By SARA CONE BRYANT (*Mrs. Theodore F. Borst*).

"Americanism," says Mrs. Borst, "needs to be taught as definitely as do geography and arithmetic. The grade teachers are doing splendid work for patriotism, with songs and recitations, story telling, and talks on civic virtues. I have tried to give them something more definite and coördinated, something that will serve as a real textbook on 'Being an American.'"

## STORIES OF PATRIOTISM.

Edited by NORMA H. DEMING, and KATHARINE I. BEMIS.

A series of stirring tales of patriotic deeds by Americans from the time of the colonists to the present. There are also stories about famous heroes of our Allies in the Great War.

## THE PATRIOTIC READER.

Edited by KATHARINE I. BEMIS, MATHILDE E. HOLTZ, and HENRY L. SMITH.

The selections cover the history of our country from Colonial times. A distinguishing feature is the freshness of material and the admirable arrangement. The book gives one a familiarity with literature that presents the highest ideals of freedom, justice, and liberty.

## THE LITTLE BOOK OF THE FLAG.

By EVA MARCH TAPPAN.

In her own entertaining style, Miss Tappan has written the story of Our Flag. She tells children how to behave toward the flag, in a fashion that makes such behavior a sacred duty. There are selections for Reading and Memorizing.

## A COURSE IN CITIZENSHIP AND PATRIOTISM.

Edited by E. L. CABOT, F. F. ANDREWS, F. E. COE, M. HILL, and M. McSKIMMON.

Good citizenship grows out of love of country and in turn promotes the spirit of internationalism. This book teaches how to develop these qualities most effectually.

## AMERICANIZATION AND CITIZENSHIP.

By HANSON HART WEBSTER.

"Well calculated to inculcate love for America, especially among the foreign born. This is to be desired at this time more than ever before." — *His Eminence, James Cardinal Gibbons.*

---

## HOUGHTON MIFFLIN COMPANY